Printed in the USA
CPSIA information can be obtained
at www.ICGtesting.com
LVHW061235260124
769744LV00001BA/1

מְגִלַּת אֶסְתֵּר

The Devash
Megillat Esther

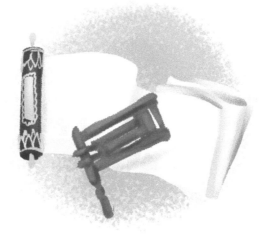

Shoshanna Lockshin, Efrayim Unterman,
and the Devash team

With illustrations by Rivka Tsinman

HADAR PRESS
NEW YORK

The Devash Megillat Esther

Translation and explanations by
Shoshanna Lockshin
Rabbi Efrayim Unterman

With contributions from
Rabbi Dr. Jason Rogoff
Dr. Jeremy Tabick

Illustrations by Rivka Tsinman
Design by Jen Klor

Library of Congress Catalog Number: 2024930456

Hadar Press
The Hadar Institute
212 West 93rd Street
New York, NY 10025

HADAR PRESS   www.hadar.org

Contents

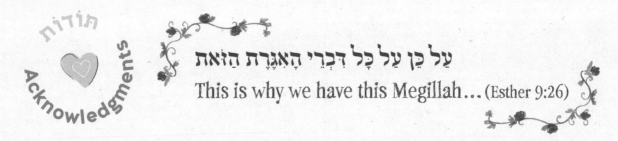

תוֹדוֹת

Acknowledgments

עַל כֵּן עַל כָּל דִּבְרֵי הָאִגֶּרֶת הַזֹּאת

This is why we have this Megillah… (Esther 9:26)

The Devash Megillat Esther tells a familiar and magical story, and also invites children to learn substantive texts and think deeply about challenging questions. It's no simple thing to layer those together, and it took a huge collaborative effort from extremely dedicated and talented individuals.

Jeremy Tabick and Jason Rogoff did research and created first drafts for most of the content in this book. Rivka Tsinman created the beautiful illustrations, and Jen Klor created the design and layout. Thank you for being such incredible partners. Each of you ought to be led on the king's horse through the streets of Shushan.

Debora Corman did copyediting, and Ari Adler checked the vowelization and punctuation we added to Hebrew texts. Avi Killip, Sam Greenberg, and Elisheva Urbas were always available to offer their time, administrative support, and wisdom. Thank you for taking this book to new levels of excellence.

Devash started off as Ethan Tucker's dream for initiating young readers into the world of parashah study. Thanks to his vision, guidance, and frequent content contributions, together with extraordinary support from The Zalik Foundation, Devash became a weekly parashah magazine reaching tens of thousands of Jewish children. Chana Kupetz made content contributions and, together with Mara Braunfeld, helped us develop the voice of Devash and ensured it reached the hands of educators, parents, and kids. Elie Kaunfer, Avi Killip, and Jeff Stein put this team together and have kept Hadar thriving. Thank you for laying the groundwork that made this book possible.

This project would not exist without the financial support of The Zalik Foundation, The William Davidson Foundation, The Wexner Foundation, and other donors. We are so thankful, and we're humbled by your generosity and kindness.

With heartfelt gratitude to you all,
Shoshanna Lockshin
Efrayim Unterman

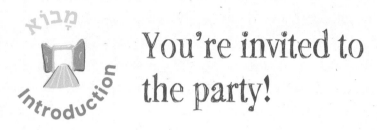

מָבוֹא
Introduction

You're invited to the party!

In *The Devash Megillat Esther*, you'll be able to learn the text of the Book of Esther together with commentaries from two thousand years of Jewish tradition. We picked these out to help you notice interesting questions about the Biblical text, spark your thinking about Jewish values, and, most importantly, invite you to ask questions and consider multiple perspectives.

Learning Torah is for all Jews, no matter how old you are or how much you have already learned. If you're comfortable with Hebrew text, great! There are lots of opportunities to learn the Megillah and its commentaries in their original language. And if you're more comfortable with English, also great! Everything in this book is in English, too, and includes plenty of clear explanations.

How do I use this book?

If you're learning, there's no wrong way! You can use it to follow along at a Megillah reading on Purim. You can read and discuss a section together with family and friends. Or you can spend just a few minutes to think about any text, question, or illustration that grabs you. Learning happens in different ways across a lifetime. We hope you'll be able to return to these pages at your own pace and in your own way for many years.

A note about the translation

Like the rest of the Tanakh (Bible), the Book of Esther was originally written for adults. But we still want kids to read and learn it. So if you're looking for the most literal and academically rigorous translation of Megillat Esther... we didn't do that here. Instead, our translation balances loyalty to the Hebrew text with sensitivity to a young audience. For example, when the Hebrew sentence structure or meaning is confusing, the English version is sometimes written more simply (e.g., 6:6 on page 65 or 8:12 on page 86).

בְּרָכוֹת
Blessings

These three בְּרָכוֹת (berakhot, blessings) are said by the reader before starting the Megillah reading. Everyone who's able should stand for the berakhot, say "amen," and then listen to the whole Megillah without interrupting.

Blessed are You, God our Lord, Ruler of the world, Who has made us holy with God's commandments, and commanded us about reading the Megillah.	בָּרוּךְ אַתָּה יהוה אֱלֹהֵינוּ מֶלֶךְ הָעוֹלָם אֲשֶׁר קִדְּשָׁנוּ בְּמִצְוֹתָיו וְצִוָּנוּ עַל מִקְרָא מְגִלָּה.
Blessed are You, God our Lord, Ruler of the world, Who made miracles for our ancestors in those days at this time.	בָּרוּךְ אַתָּה יהוה אֱלֹהֵינוּ מֶלֶךְ הָעוֹלָם שֶׁעָשָׂה נִסִּים לַאֲבוֹתֵינוּ בַּיָּמִים הָהֵם בַּזְּמַן הַזֶּה.
Blessed are You, God our Lord, Ruler of the world, Who has kept us alive, sustained us, and brought us to this time.	בָּרוּךְ אַתָּה יהוה אֱלֹהֵינוּ מֶלֶךְ הָעוֹלָם שֶׁהֶחֱיָנוּ וְקִיְּמָנוּ וְהִגִּיעָנוּ לַזְּמַן הַזֶּה.

Amen!

CHAPTER 1 פֶּרֶק א

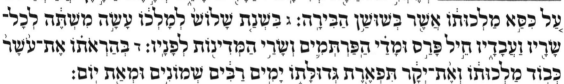

כִּימֵי אֲחַשְׁוֵרוֹשׁ הוּא אֲחַשְׁוֵרוֹשׁ הַמֹּלֵךְ מֵהֹדּוּ וְעַד־כּוּשׁ שֶׁבַע
וְעֶשְׂרִים וּמֵאָה מְדִינָה: ב בַּיָּמִים הָהֵם כְּשֶׁבֶת הַמֶּלֶךְ אֲחַשְׁוֵרוֹשׁ
עַל כִּסֵּא מַלְכוּתוֹ אֲשֶׁר בְּשׁוּשַׁן הַבִּירָה: ג בִּשְׁנַת שָׁלוֹשׁ לְמָלְכוֹ עָשָׂה מִשְׁתֶּה לְכָל־
שָׂרָיו וַעֲבָדָיו חֵיל פָּרַס וּמָדַי הַפַּרְתְּמִים וְשָׂרֵי הַמְּדִינוֹת לְפָנָיו: ד בְּהַרְאֹתוֹ אֶת־עֹשֶׁר
כְּבוֹד מַלְכוּתוֹ וְאֶת־יְקָר תִּפְאֶרֶת גְּדוּלָּתוֹ יָמִים רַבִּים שְׁמוֹנִים וּמְאַת יוֹם:

1 It was in the days of Ahashverosh–who ruled from Hodu to Kush, 127 provinces. 2 The following story takes place in those days, when King Ahashverosh sat on his royal throne in Shushan the capital. 3 In his third year of being king, he made a banquet for all his officers and subjects–the army of Persia and Madai, and the nobles of the provinces. 4 This was when he showed off the wealth and glory of his kingdom and greatness. This banquet lasted for a long time: 180 days!

שְׁאֵלוֹת

Scavenger Hunt

FIND THE ANSWERS IN CHAPTER 1!

1. How many days did Ahashverosh's parties last?

2. What word matches an item on the Seder table?

3. Who throws a party?

4. Why did Vashti refuse to come to Ahashverosh's party?

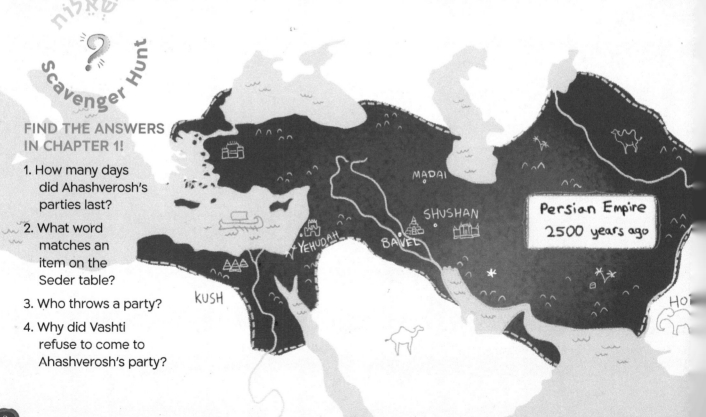

MADAI

SHUSHAN

Persian Empire 2500 years ago

YEHUDAH

BAVEL

KUSH

HO

ה וּבִמְלוֹאת הַיָּמִים הָאֵלֶּה עָשָׂה הַמֶּלֶךְ לְכָל־הָעָם הַנִּמְצְאִים בְּשׁוּשַׁן הַבִּירָה לְמִגָּדוֹל וְעַד־קָטָן מִשְׁתֶּה שִׁבְעַת יָמִים בַּחֲצַר גִּנַּת בִּיתַן הַמֶּלֶךְ:

5 At the end of these days, the king made another banquet in the palace garden for all the people in Shushan–from great to small–for seven days.

Ahashverosh was a foolish king.

Disagree!

○ Everyone seems afraid of him and willing to listen to his decrees.

○ He's king over a lot of provinces. That can't have been an accident.

○ In the end, he sees that Haman is a bad guy.

○ Being mean doesn't mean he wasn't clever about it. When people are cunning about doing evil, that's pretty scary.

Agree!

○ He's very impulsive, and he parties way too much. He should take his decisions more seriously.

○ He listens to people like Haman, so how smart can he have been?

○ He treats people—like Vashti, young women, Esther, and the Jewish people—really terribly. Sounds foolish to me.

Pasuk 5
After Ahashverosh hosted a party for people from the far-off parts of his kingdom, he hosted the Shushan residents for a party of their own. Was this a good idea?

Talmud Bavli Megillah 12a

תלמוד בבלי מגילה דף יב עמוד א

Rav and Shmuel disagreed.

One said: Ahashverosh was a clever king.

And the other one said: Ahashverosh was a foolish king.

The argument that he was clever is that it was good to first invite his faraway subjects, because for the residents of his own city, he could make it up to them any time.

The argument that he was foolish is that he should have invited the residents of his own city first, so he could count on their support if his faraway subjects were to rebel.

רַב וּשְׁמוּאֵל, חַד אָמַר: מֶלֶךְ פִּיקֵחַ הָיָה, וְחַד אָמַר: מֶלֶךְ טִיפֵּשׁ הָיָה.

מַאן דְּאָמַר מֶלֶךְ פִּיקֵחַ הָיָה—שַׁפִּיר עֲבַד דְּקָרֵיב רְחִיקָא בְּרֵישָׁא, דִּבְנֵי מָאתֵיה כָּל אֵימַת דְּבָעֵי מְפַיֵּיס לְהוּ.

וּמַאן דְּאָמַר טִיפֵּשׁ הָיָה—דְּאִיבְּעֵי לֵיה לְקָרוֹבֵי בְּנֵי מָאתֵיה בְּרֵישָׁא, דְּאִי מָרְדוּ בֵּיה הָנָךְ, הָנֵי הֲווֹ קָיְימִי בַּהֲדֵיה.

It seems the Talmud believes that some group of people is definitely going to be upset. The question is: What's best? Does it make the most sense to let his local, hometown subjects be upset (by making the first party for the faraway people), and then try to make it up to them later? Or does it make the most sense to let the faraway subjects be upset (by making the first party for the local people), and then rely on the support of his local subjects?

In the end, Ahashverosh chooses to give a party to the faraway subjects first.

- What do you think? Is that clever or foolish?
- Can you think of other evidence for Ahashverosh being clever or being foolish?
- What would you do? Are there other things Ahashverosh could have done?
- What would you feel if you were one of Ahashverosh's local subjects and you got your own party but had to wait for it?

ו חוּר כַּרְפַּס וּתְכֵלֶת אָחוּז בְּחַבְלֵי־בוּץ וְאַרְגָּמָן עַל־גְּלִילֵי כֶסֶף וְעַמּוּדֵי שֵׁשׁ מִטּוֹת זָהָב וָכֶסֶף עַל רִצְפַת בַּהַט־וָשֵׁשׁ וְדַר וְסֹחָרֶת: ז וְהַשְׁקוֹת בִּכְלֵי זָהָב וְכֵלִים מִכֵּלִים שׁוֹנִים וְיֵין מַלְכוּת רָב כְּיַד הַמֶּלֶךְ: ח וְהַשְּׁתִיָּה כַדָּת אֵין אֹנֵס כִּי־כֵן יִסַּד הַמֶּלֶךְ עַל כָּל־רַב בֵּיתוֹ לַעֲשׂוֹת כִּרְצוֹן אִישׁ־וָאִישׁ:

פסוק ז - PASUK 7
וְכֵלִים מִכֵּלִים שׁוֹנִים The words (and the keilim [vessels] were from different kinds of vessels) are read in the sad tune of Megillat Eikhah.

6 It was decorated with luxurious curtains made of *karpas* and *tekhelet* (special fabric), hanging on ropes tied to silver rods and marble pillars. There were couches of gold and silver, on a fancy floor of special stones. 7 There was as much wine as the king pleased, served in golden vessels—and the *keilim* (vessels) were from different kinds of vessels. 8 The drinking was to order—no limits—because that's what the king told all of his great house, to get the guests whatever they wanted.

Pasuk 7
What does it mean to say that the כֵּלִים (keilim, vessels) were "from different kinds of vessels"?

Yalkut Shimoni on Na"kh

"From different kinds of vessels"—Ahashverosh's keilim were the most beautiful in the world, but the keilim from the Beit HaMikdash (Holy Temple) were even more beautiful.... Any time Ahashverosh's keilim were near the ones from the Beit HaMikdash, his would change into lead.

ילקוט שמעוני נ"ך תתרמ"ח

"מִכֵּלִים שׁוֹנִים"—כֵּלָיו נָאִים מִשֶּׁל כָּל הָעוֹלָם, וּכְלֵי בֵּית הַמִּקְדָּשׁ הָיוּ נָאוֹת מִכֵּלָיו.... כָּל זְמַן שֶׁמַּרְאִים כֵּלָיו עִם כְּלֵי בֵּית הַמִּקְדָּשׁ מִשְׁתַּנִּין וְנַעֲשׂוּ כַּעוֹפֶרֶת.

This midrash suggests that there were keilim at this party that really were quite different, unusual, and more special than any other keilim in the world. That's because they were the keilim of the Beit HaMikdash! According to this midrash, Ahashverosh got them from the people who destroyed the first Beit HaMikdash and stole its keilim not long before his party.

- If Ahashverosh were using keilim stolen from the Beit HaMikdash, what would that teach us about him?

- Does this midrash change your understanding of what was going on at Ahashverosh's party? How so?

The midrash notices something else too. The word שׁוֹנִים (shonim, different) can also mean "changed." So the midrash suggests that not only were there the different and special keilim from the Beit HaMikdash, but the other vessels at the party changed from gold to lead when they were in the presence of the Beit HaMikdash keilim.

- Why would the other beautiful vessels change into something worse when they were in the presence of the Beit HaMikdash keilim?

- TRY IT OUT! Go outside on a sunny day, and turn on a flashlight. Does the flashlight seem like it's doing anything at all? How does this help you understand our midrash?

ט גַּם וַשְׁתִּי הַמַּלְכָּה עָשְׂתָה מִשְׁתֵּה נָשִׁים בֵּית הַמַּלְכוּת אֲשֶׁר לַמֶּלֶךְ אֲחַשְׁוֵרוֹשׁ: י בַּיּוֹם הַשְּׁבִיעִי כְּטוֹב לֵב־הַמֶּלֶךְ בַּיָּיִן אָמַר לִמְהוּמָן בִּזְּתָא חַרְבוֹנָא בִּגְתָא וַאֲבַגְתָא זֵתַר וְכַרְכַּס שִׁבְעַת הַסָּרִיסִים הַמְשָׁרְתִים אֶת־פְּנֵי הַמֶּלֶךְ אֲחַשְׁוֵרוֹשׁ: יא לְהָבִיא אֶת־וַשְׁתִּי הַמַּלְכָּה לִפְנֵי הַמֶּלֶךְ בְּכֶתֶר מַלְכוּת לְהַרְאוֹת הָעַמִּים וְהַשָּׂרִים אֶת־יָפְיָהּ כִּי־טוֹבַת מַרְאֶה הִיא:

9 Queen Vashti also made a banquet for women, in the royal palace of King Ahashverosh. 10 On the seventh day, when the king was very drunk, he told his seven attendants—Mehuman, Bizzeta, Harvona, Bigta, Avagta, Zetar, and Kharkas— 11 to bring Queen Vashti to him wearing a royal crown, to show off her beauty to the people and the nobles; for she looked good.

יב וַתְּמָאֵ֞ן הַמַּלְכָּ֣ה וַשְׁתִּ֗י לָבוֹא֙ בִּדְבַ֣ר הַמֶּ֔לֶךְ אֲשֶׁ֖ר בְּיַ֣ד הַסָּרִיסִ֑ים וַיִּקְצֹ֤ף הַמֶּ֙לֶךְ֙ מְאֹ֔ד וַחֲמָת֖וֹ בָּעֲרָ֥ה בֽוֹ:

12 Queen Vashti refused to come. The king was furious, and his anger burned inside him.

R. Alshikh concludes:

He was a stupid king not only because he told Vashti to come in such an inappropriate way, but he also got uncontrollably angry about it.	מֶלֶךְ טִפֵּשׁ הָיָה כִּי גַם שֶׁלֹּא יְבַצֵּר מִמֶּנּוּ כִּי שָׁאַל שֶׁלֹּא כַּהֹגֶן קָצַף מְאֹד.

- Was Ahashverosh clever or foolish? How does perek 1 of Megillat Esther help shape our understanding of Ahashverosh for the rest of the story?

- Can you think of other places where Ahashverosh was not kind to the women around him? What does this tell us about Ahashverosh?

- How does Ahashverosh's behavior in this perek relate to his attitude toward the Jewish people later on when Haman asks for permission to destroy them?

Pasuk 12
Why didn't Vashti come to Ahashverosh's party? The Megillah doesn't say!

R. Moshe Alshikh suggests that it was because Ahashverosh's demand was inappropriate:

R. Moshe Alshikh (Eretz Yisrael, 500 years ago)

Besides the stupid wickedness of summoning her in a foolish and offensive way... he did not ask her to come with her own maidservants in a manner befitting a queen such as herself... for it is not in accordance with her honor to be forced to come like a prisoner in the hands of her husband's servants.... And he also did not ask her to come of her own consent and free will, but rather he tried to force her like a slave that he can command whether she wants to or not.

משאת משה

הִנֵּה זוּלַת הוֹלְלוּת רָעַת מְצִיאוּת הַשְּׁלִיחוּת לַהֲבִיאָהּ לִידֵי בִּזָּיוֹן... לֹא שָׁלַח אֵלֶיהָ לֵאמֹר תָּבֹא עִם נַעֲרוֹתֶיהָ כְּדֶרֶךְ מַלְכָּה כָּמוֹהָ.... שֶׁאֵינוֹ לְפִי כְּבוֹדָהּ תָּבֹא כְּנִצוֹרָה בְּיַד שְׁלוּחֵי הַבַּעַל מְשָׁרְתָיו... שֶׁלֹּא שָׁלַח לְבַקֵּשׁ מִמֶּנָּה תָּבֹא אֶל הַמֶּלֶךְ כְּבָאָה בְּרָצוֹן וּבְחִירָה רַק שֶׁיְבִיאוּהָ כְּעֶבֶד מֶלֶךְ אוֹ שִׁפְחָה שֶׁיְצַוֶּה הַמֶּלֶךְ לַהֲבִיאָהּ מִדַּעְתָּהּ וְשֶׁלֹּא מִדַּעְתָּהּ.

- According to R. Alshikh, why didn't Vashti agree to come to Ahashverosh's party?

- R. Alshikh points out that Vashti should have been given her own choice whether to come to his party or not. This is called asking for consent. Why is it so important to allow people to make their own choices about whether they listen to you or not?

R. Alshikh continues:

Shouldn't a king be better than this? Shouldn't he see and realize that his request was nasty? What woman would listen to this kind of demand?...

Quite the opposite, he should have thanked her that she didn't come under these circumstances. So why did he get so angry when he was the one who was inappropriate?

הֲלֹא לַאֲמִתַּת זֶה רָאוּי לַמֶּלֶךְ אַל יְהִי סָבָל וְיַשְׁקֵיף וְיֵרָא כִּי קָשֶׁה כִּשְׁאוֹל שְׁאֶלָתוֹ הָרָעָה וּמִי הָאִשָּׁה תִּשְׁמַע אֵלָיו לַדָּבָר הַזֶּה... וְאַדְּרַבָּה עָלָיו לְהַחֲזִיק לָהּ טוֹבָה שֶׁלֹּא בָאָה וְלָמָּה זֶה קָצַף מְאֹד עִם הֱיוֹת שֶׁשָּׁאַל שֶׁלֹּא כַהֹגֶן.

- According to R. Alshikh, did Vashti need a reason to say "no" to Ahashverosh? Why?

- Look at pasuk 11. What do you notice? What seems to be Ahashverosh's way of looking at Vashti? What do you think about that, and what does this teach us about Ahashverosh?

- Why should Ahashverosh have thanked Vashti for refusing to come? What should Ahashverosh have learned from Vashti?

יג וַיֹּאמֶר הַמֶּלֶךְ לַחֲכָמִים יֹדְעֵי הָעִתִּים כִּי־כֵן דְּבַר הַמֶּלֶךְ לִפְנֵי כָּל־יֹדְעֵי דָּת וָדִין: יד וְהַקָּרֹב אֵלָיו כַּרְשְׁנָא שֵׁתָר אַדְמָתָא תַרְשִׁישׁ מֶרֶס מַרְסְנָא מְמוּכָן שִׁבְעַת שָׂרֵי פָּרַס וּמָדַי רֹאֵי פְּנֵי הַמֶּלֶךְ הַיֹּשְׁבִים רִאשֹׁנָה בַּמַּלְכוּת: טו כְּדָת מַה־לַּעֲשׂוֹת בַּמַּלְכָּה וַשְׁתִּי עַל אֲשֶׁר לֹא־עָשְׂתָה אֶת־מַאֲמַר הַמֶּלֶךְ אֲחַשְׁוֵרוֹשׁ בְּיַד הַסָּרִיסִים: טז וַיֹּאמֶר מְמוּכָן לִפְנֵי הַמֶּלֶךְ וְהַשָּׂרִים לֹא עַל־הַמֶּלֶךְ לְבַדּוֹ עָוְתָה וַשְׁתִּי הַמַּלְכָּה כִּי עַל־כָּל־הַשָּׂרִים וְעַל־כָּל־הָעַמִּים אֲשֶׁר בְּכָל־מְדִינוֹת הַמֶּלֶךְ אֲחַשְׁוֵרוֹשׁ: יז כִּי־יֵצֵא דְבַר־הַמַּלְכָּה עַל־כָּל־הַנָּשִׁים לְהַבְזוֹת בַּעְלֵיהֶן בְּעֵינֵיהֶן בְּאָמְרָם הַמֶּלֶךְ אֲחַשְׁוֵרוֹשׁ אָמַר לְהָבִיא אֶת־וַשְׁתִּי הַמַּלְכָּה לְפָנָיו וְלֹא־בָאָה: יח וְהַיּוֹם הַזֶּה תֹּאמַרְנָה שָׂרוֹת פָּרַס־וּמָדַי אֲשֶׁר שָׁמְעוּ אֶת־דְּבַר הַמַּלְכָּה לְכֹל שָׂרֵי הַמֶּלֶךְ וּכְדַי בִּזָּיוֹן וָקָצֶף:

13 The king spoke with wise advisors (because the king would often consult people who knew the law). 14 These were Karshena, Sheitar, Admata, Tarshish, Meres, Marsena, and Memukhan, who were his closest advisors, the seven nobles of Persia and Madai who would sit closest to the king. 15 They had to figure out: What should be done with Queen Vashti for not obeying the word of the king? 16 Memukhan spoke up and said to the king and nobles, "Queen Vashti's crime wasn't just against the king, but also against all the nobles and all the peoples in all the provinces of King Ahashverosh! 17 When word of the queen goes out, all women will disrespect their husbands—especially when people say that King Ahashverosh told Queen Vashti to come, but she didn't. 18 Even today the noblewomen of Persia and Madai who heard what the queen said to all the king's noblemen will talk about it, and there will be disrespect and anger!

יט אִם־עַל־הַמֶּלֶךְ טוֹב יֵצֵא דְבַר־מַלְכוּת מִלְּפָנָיו וְיִכָּתֵב בְּדָתֵי פָרַס־וּמָדַי וְלֹא יַעֲבוֹר אֲשֶׁר לֹא־תָבוֹא וַשְׁתִּי לִפְנֵי הַמֶּלֶךְ אֲחַשְׁוֵרוֹשׁ וּמַלְכוּתָהּ יִתֵּן הַמֶּלֶךְ לִרְעוּתָהּ הַטּוֹבָה מִמֶּנָּה: כ וְנִשְׁמַע פִּתְגָם הַמֶּלֶךְ אֲשֶׁר־יַעֲשֶׂה בְּכָל־מַלְכוּתוֹ כִּי רַבָּה הִיא וְכָל־הַנָּשִׁים יִתְּנוּ יְקָר לְבַעְלֵיהֶן לְמִגָּדוֹל וְעַד־קָטָן: כא וַיִּיטַב הַדָּבָר בְּעֵינֵי הַמֶּלֶךְ וְהַשָּׂרִים וַיַּעַשׂ הַמֶּלֶךְ כִּדְבַר מְמוּכָן: כב וַיִּשְׁלַח סְפָרִים אֶל־כָּל־מְדִינוֹת הַמֶּלֶךְ אֶל־מְדִינָה וּמְדִינָה כִּכְתָבָהּ וְאֶל־עַם וָעָם כִּלְשׁוֹנוֹ לִהְיוֹת כָּל־אִישׁ שֹׂרֵר בְּבֵיתוֹ וּמְדַבֵּר כִּלְשׁוֹן עַמּוֹ:

19 "If it pleases Your Majesty, send a royal decree and let it be written forever in the laws of Persia and Madai: 'Because Vashti wouldn't come before King Ahashverosh, the king will give her crown to someone more obedient.' 20 Your Majesty's decree will be heard throughout the kingdom–far and wide–and all women will give honor to their husbands, great and small." 21 This seemed good to the king and the nobles, and the king did what Memukhan suggested. 22 He sent scrolls to all his provinces–to each one in its own script, and to each people in their own language–declaring that every man should rule his home and speak the way he wants.

Pasuk 19
What happened to Vashti?
The Megillah doesn't say!

Here are two opinions from our פַּרְשָׁנִים (parshanim, commentators):

רש"י	רשב"ם
וּלְכָךְ נֶהֱרְגָה.	יְגָרְשֶׁנָּה מִבֵּיתוֹ.
Rashi (France, 1,000 years ago)	**Rashbam (France, 950 years ago)**
She was executed.	Ahashverosh sent her away from his palace forever.

- Vashti is never mentioned again in the Megillah. How does this support Rashi's reading?

- What evidence in the Megillah text can you find to support Rashbam's reading?

- The phrase in pasuk 19 אֲשֶׁר לֹא תָבוֹא וַשְׁתִּי could mean "because Vashti wouldn't come" (that's how we translated it), or it could mean "Vashti shall never again come." Which translation do you think works better with Rashi, and which with Rashbam?

- According to each view, what might the Megillah be teaching us? How might each one add to our understanding of the story that follows?

שְׁאֵלוֹת

?

Scavenger Hunt

FIND THE
ANSWERS
IN CHAPTER 2!

1. Who was Mordekhai's great-grandfather?

2. What was Esther's other name?

3. How frequently did Mordekhai check on Esther?

4. When was Esther taken to King Ahashverosh?

QUEEN
WANTED!
Must Look
Good!

פְּשָׁט

Reading the Verses

Pesukim 2–4

- What do you notice?

- How are the women being chosen? Does this system make sense?

- The focus seems to be entirely on how the women look. Do external appearances matter to you? When, and how much?

- Avraham's servant found Yitzhak a wife by seeing if she would give water to him and his camels (Bereishit chapter 24). How does this compare to the way that Ahashverosh's servants found him a wife? What was Avraham's servant looking for? What can you learn from the differences between these stories?

CHAPTER 2 פֶּרֶק ב

הַדְּבָרִים הָאֵלֶּה כְּשֹׁךְ חֲמַת הַמֶּלֶךְ אֲחַשְׁוֵרוֹשׁ זָכַר אֶת־וַשְׁתִּי וְאֵת אֲשֶׁר־עָשָׂתָה וְאֵת אֲשֶׁר־נִגְזַר עָלֶיהָ: ב וַיֹּאמְרוּ נַעֲרֵי־הַמֶּלֶךְ מְשָׁרְתָיו יְבַקְשׁוּ לַמֶּלֶךְ נְעָרוֹת בְּתוּלוֹת טוֹבוֹת מַרְאֶה: ג וְיַפְקֵד הַמֶּלֶךְ פְּקִידִים בְּכָל־מְדִינוֹת מַלְכוּתוֹ וְיִקְבְּצוּ אֶת־כָּל־נַעֲרָה־בְתוּלָה טוֹבַת מַרְאֶה אֶל־שׁוּשַׁן הַבִּירָה אֶל־בֵּית הַנָּשִׁים אֶל־יַד הֵגֶא סְרִיס הַמֶּלֶךְ שֹׁמֵר הַנָּשִׁים וְנָתוֹן תַּמְרֻקֵיהֶן: ד וְהַנַּעֲרָה אֲשֶׁר תִּיטַב בְּעֵינֵי הַמֶּלֶךְ תִּמְלֹךְ תַּחַת וַשְׁתִּי וַיִּיטַב הַדָּבָר בְּעֵינֵי הַמֶּלֶךְ וַיַּעַשׂ כֵּן:

1 After all this, when King Ahashverosh's anger had died down, he remembered Vashti, what she had done, and what had been decreed against her. 2 The king's servants said, "Let's find the king some young women who look good. 3 Appoint officers in every province of the kingdom, and have them gather all the young women who look good. Bring them to Shushan to the house of Hegai, boss of the women, and put makeup on them. 4 And whichever young woman seems good to Your Majesty will become queen instead of Vashti." The king liked this idea, and he did it.

ה אִישׁ יְהוּדִי הָיָה בְּשׁוּשַׁן הַבִּירָה וּשְׁמוֹ מָרְדֳּכַי בֶּן יָאִיר בֶּן־שִׁמְעִי בֶּן־
קִישׁ אִישׁ יְמִינִי: ו אֲשֶׁר הָגְלָה מִירוּשָׁלַיִם עִם־הַגֹּלָה אֲשֶׁר הָגְלְתָה
עִם יְכָנְיָה מֶלֶךְ־יְהוּדָה אֲשֶׁר הֶגְלָה נְבוּכַדְנֶצַּר מֶלֶךְ בָּבֶל:

PASUK 5 - ה פסוק
This pasuk is first recited by the קָהָל
(kahal, community) and then by the reader.

PASUK 6 - ו פסוק
This pasuk is read in the sad tune of
Megillat Eikhah.

5 There was a *Yehudi* in Shushan the capital, and his name was Mordekhai son of Yair son of Shimi son of Kish, a *Yemini*. 6 He was exiled from Yerushalayim with all the exiles who were kicked out with Yekhoniah, king of Yehudah, by Nevukhadnetzar, king of Bavel.

In today's Hebrew, Yehudi means "Jewish." This is because, like Mordekhai, Jewish people used to live where shevet Yehudah was and were exiled together (even if we originally came from a number of different tribes). So you can come from different tribes but still be called "Jewish." That's why we'll be translating Yehudi as "Jewish" for the rest of the Megillah. See if you can find all the places where Mordekhai is called "Mordekhai ha-Yehudi"!

Pasuk 5

Mordekhai is called אִישׁ יְהוּדִי (ish Yehudi). This means "a man from Yehudah." But he's also called אִישׁ יְמִינִי (ish Yemini, a man from Yemin), which means from the שֵׁבֶט (shevet, tribe) of Binyamin.

Which shevet is Mordekhai actually from: Yehudah or Binyamin?

We get a clue from his great-grandfather's name: Kish. This was also the name of the father of King Shaul, who came from shevet Binyamin (look at Shmuel Alef 10:21).

The connections between King Shaul and Mordekhai go deeper. Shaul had a battle against Agag, the king of Amalek (Shmuel Alef 15). And who in the Megillah is called "the Agagi"? Haman (Esther 3:1)!

> In the Purim story, Mordekhai's fight against Haman can be a continuation of Shaul's fight against Agag.

> • How does it change what this story means to us to think that there are forces of evil we have to fight against for hundreds or thousands of years?

But if Mordekhai really came from shevet Binyanim, why was he called Yehudi? Here's one answer:

R. Yosef Kara (France, 900 years ago) — ר' יוסף קרא

Anywhere the tribe of Yehudah was exiled, the tribe of Binyamin was exiled with them, because their land was close to each other.

בְּכָל מָקוֹם שֶׁגָּלוּ שֵׁבֶט יְהוּדָה גָּלָה שֵׁבֶט בִּנְיָמִין עִמָּהֶן, לְפִי שֶׁנַּחֲלָתָן הָיְתָה סְמוּכָה זוֹ לָזוֹ.

> According to R. Kara, shevet Binyamin was in exile together with Shevet Yehudah (see Melakhim Bet 24:14–15).

> • Why would being exiled together or living together mean that someone from Binyamin can be called a Yehudi? What does that teach us about what it means to be a Yehudi? Is it more about what tribe you're from, or is it something else?

ז וַיְהִי אֹמֵן אֶת־הֲדַסָּה הִיא אֶסְתֵּר בַּת־דֹּדוֹ כִּי אֵין לָהּ אָב וָאֵם וְהַנַּעֲרָה יְפַת־תֹּאַר וְטוֹבַת מַרְאֶה וּבְמוֹת אָבִיהָ וְאִמָּהּ לְקָחָהּ מָרְדֳּכַי לוֹ לְבַת:

7 He raised Hadassah, who is Esther, his cousin, because she didn't have a father or mother. She appeared beautiful and she was good-looking, and when her father and mother died, Mordekhai took her as a daughter.

דִּקְדּוּק
Grammar

Pasuk 5
Mor-de-khai or Mor-do-khai?

According to the Minhat Shai (Italy, 450 years ago), different manuscripts and editions of Tanakh give slightly different נְקוּדוֹת (nekudot, vowels) for this name. So it seems the correct way to pronounce it is up for debate!

But in the oldest complete version of the Tanakh, which was written in Cairo about 1,000 years ago, the nekudot on this name are מָרְדֳּכַי. That's a hataf-kamatz under the letter dalet, and it's pronounced like a short o, which would make the name: Mord**o**khai. The Minhat Shai concludes that this is probably the best way to pronounce the name. But if you're in shul and you hear מָרְדְּכַי (Mord**e**khai), with a sheva (like a short i sound) under the dalet, that's still okay!

Midrash

Pasuk 7
What's important about Mordekhai adopting Esther?

Esther Rabbah 6:1

"Happy are those who observe the law, who act with righteousness all the time" (Tehillim 106:3)—R. Tarfon and his students tried to determine: Who acts with righteousness all the time? If you say it's scribes and teachers, do they not take a break to eat, drink, and sleep? Or could it be people who write tefillin and mezuzot? But do they not eat, drink, and sleep?

So who acts with righteousness all the time? You must say: It's a person who raises an orphan in their home.

אסתר רבה ו:א

"אַשְׁרֵי שֹׁמְרֵי מִשְׁפָּט עֹשֵׂה צְדָקָה בְכָל עֵת" (תהלים קו:ג)— נִמְנוּ בַּעֲלִיַּת רַבִּי טַרְפוֹן וְאָמְרוּ אֵיזֶה הוּא שֶׁעוֹשֶׂה צְדָקָה בְּכָל עֵת, אִם תֹּאמַר אֵלּוּ סוֹפְרִים וּמַשְׁנִים, אֵינָן לֹא אוֹכְלִים וְלֹא שׁוֹתִין וְלֹא יְשֵׁנִים, אֶלָּא אֵלּוּ כּוֹתְבֵי תְּפִלִּין וּמְזוּזוֹת, אֵינָן לֹא אוֹכְלִים וְלֹא שׁוֹתִין וְלֹא יְשֵׁנִים, אֶלָּא אֵיזֶהוּ עוֹשֶׂה צְדָקָה בְּכָל עֵת, הֱוֵי אוֹמֵר זֶה הַמְגַדֵּל יָתוֹם בְּתוֹךְ בֵּיתוֹ.

According to this midrash, adopting orphans is a kind of tzedakah that never stops for a moment, and that makes it better than other kinds of tzedakah, and even better than learning and teaching Torah or writing tefillin and mezuzot!

- All parents constantly do kind things for their kids. What makes foster parents special?
- What might this teach us about the relationship that Mordekhai and Esther had?

The midrash continues on to suggest that God saved the Jewish people from Haman's decree because Mordekhai did the great act of adopting Esther!

- Why is adoption so great that it can save the entire nation?
- How is every adoption like an act of salvation?

The other Sages think that Hadassah is her real name, and Esther was added.

 2   **R. Yehudah** thinks that's because Esther connects to the Hebrew word סָתַר (satar, hid), and she hid her Jewish identity in the story. Another gemara (Bavli Hulin 139b) suggests that it connects to when God says, "I will hide My face" (Devarim 31:18) when Benei Yisrael turn away from God.

- What is so important about the way Esther hid her Jewish identity in the story?

- הֶסְתֵּר פָּנִים (hester panim, God's face being hidden) is when God acts distant from us and turns away. Being face-to-face with someone means being close to them and having them in your life. Hester panim is when God does the opposite of that. How does hester panim connect to Esther's story? How does thinking about Esther help make things better when there is hester panim? (For more on hester panim, and why God's name never appears in the Megillah, see page 55!)

 3   **R. Nehemiah** also thinks Hadassah is her real name, and Esther actually comes from a non-Jewish word! Even today, some girls are still given the Persian name Setareh, which means "star." Listen to how the words "Esther" and "Setareh" and "star" sound alike! A midrash explains:

Yalkut Shimoni on Na"kh | **ילקוט שמעוני נ"ך תרפ"ה**

"For the morning star" (Tehillim 22:1)—Why is Esther compared to the dawn? The dawn rises up and the stars sink down, and this is like Esther in Ahashverosh's house. She gave off light, and Haman and his children sunk down.

"עַל אַיֶּלֶת הַשַּׁחַר"—לָמָּה נִמְשְׁלָה אֶסְתֵּר לְשַׁחַר לוֹמַר לָךְ מָה הַשַּׁחַר עוֹלֶה וְהַכּוֹכָבִים שׁוֹקְעִים אַף אֶסְתֵּר בְּבֵית אֲחַשְׁוֵרוֹשׁ הִיא הָיְתָה מְאִירָה וְהָמָן וּבָנָיו שׁוֹקְעִין.

- Why is Esther like the dawn of light in the morning?

- Which "star" brings light in the morning? What are Hazal trying to teach us about Esther by comparing her to the sun?

מדרש
Midrash

Pasuk 7
The heroine of the Purim story is called both Hadassah and Esther! Why does she have two names?

The Gemara has three answers.

Talmud Bavli Megillah 13a

R. Meir says: Her real name was Esther. So why was she called Hadassah? Because tzaddikim (righteous people) are sometimes called hadassim (myrtle plants)....

R. Yehudah says: Her real name was Hadassah. So why was she called Esther? Because she hid (masteret) the truth about herself, as it says: "Esther didn't tell her origin" (Esther 2:20).

R. Nehemiah says: Her real name was Hadassah. So why was she called Esther? The nations of the world called her this, after Istahar.

תלמוד בבלי מגילה דף יג עמוד א

רַבִּי מֵאִיר אוֹמֵר: אֶסְתֵּר שְׁמָהּ, וְלָמָּה נִקְרָא שְׁמָהּ הֲדַסָּה? עַל שֵׁם הַצַּדִּיקִים שֶׁנִּקְרְאוּ הֲדַסִּים....

רַבִּי יְהוּדָה אוֹמֵר: הֲדַסָּה שְׁמָהּ, וְלָמָּה נִקְרֵאת שְׁמָהּ אֶסְתֵּר? עַל שֵׁם שֶׁהָיְתָה מַסְתֶּרֶת דְּבָרֶיהָ, שֶׁנֶּאֱמַר: "אֵין אֶסְתֵּר מַגֶּדֶת אֶת עַמָּהּ."

רַבִּי נְחֶמְיָה אוֹמֵר: הֲדַסָּה שְׁמָהּ, וְלָמָּה נִקְרֵאת אֶסְתֵּר? שֶׁהָיוּ אוּמּוֹת הָעוֹלָם קוֹרִין אוֹתָהּ עַל שׁוּם אִסְתַּהַר.

These Sages suggest that one of these was her real name, and an extra one was added to teach us different things about Esther.

1 **R. Meir** thinks that Esther is her real name. Hadassah was added because she was righteous, and tzaddikim are called hadassim. A midrash (Yalkut Shimoni on Na"kh 1053) explains: "כְּשֵׁם שֶׁהֲדַס רֵיחוֹ טוֹב כָּךְ הָיוּ מַעֲשֶׂיהָ טוֹבִים"—hadassim have a good smell, and Esther had good actions!"

- How are righteous actions like the good smell of hadassim? What does this teach us about Esther?

- How can your actions have an impact on others like hadassim do?

ח וַיְהִי כְּהִשָּׁמַע דְּבַר־הַמֶּלֶךְ וְדָתוֹ וּבְהִקָּבֵץ נְעָרוֹת רַבּוֹת אֶל־שׁוּשַׁן הַבִּירָה אֶל־יַד הֵגָי וַתִּלָּקַח אֶסְתֵּר אֶל־בֵּית הַמֶּלֶךְ אֶל־יַד הֵגַי שֹׁמֵר הַנָּשִׁים: ט וַתִּיטַב הַנַּעֲרָה בְעֵינָיו וַתִּשָּׂא חֶסֶד לְפָנָיו וַיְבַהֵל אֶת־תַּמְרוּקֶיהָ וְאֶת־מָנוֹתֶהָ לָתֵת לָהּ וְאֵת שֶׁבַע הַנְּעָרוֹת הָרְאֻיוֹת לָתֶת־לָהּ מִבֵּית הַמֶּלֶךְ וַיְשַׁנֶּהָ וְאֶת־נַעֲרוֹתֶיהָ לְטוֹב בֵּית הַנָּשִׁים: י לֹא־הִגִּידָה אֶסְתֵּר אֶת־עַמָּהּ וְאֶת־מוֹלַדְתָּהּ כִּי מָרְדֳּכַי צִוָּה עָלֶיהָ אֲשֶׁר לֹא־תַגִּיד: יא וּבְכָל־יוֹם וָיוֹם מָרְדֳּכַי מִתְהַלֵּךְ לִפְנֵי חֲצַר בֵּית־הַנָּשִׁים לָדַעַת אֶת־שְׁלוֹם אֶסְתֵּר וּמַה־יֵּעָשֶׂה בָּהּ: יב וּבְהַגִּיעַ תֹּר נַעֲרָה וְנַעֲרָה לָבוֹא אֶל־הַמֶּלֶךְ אֲחַשְׁוֵרוֹשׁ מִקֵּץ הֱיוֹת לָהּ כְּדָת הַנָּשִׁים שְׁנֵים עָשָׂר חֹדֶשׁ כִּי כֵּן יִמְלְאוּ יְמֵי מְרוּקֵיהֶן שִׁשָּׁה חֳדָשִׁים בְּשֶׁמֶן הַמֹּר וְשִׁשָּׁה חֳדָשִׁים בַּבְּשָׂמִים וּבְתַמְרוּקֵי הַנָּשִׁים: יג וּבָזֶה הַנַּעֲרָה בָּאָה אֶל־הַמֶּלֶךְ אֵת כָּל־אֲשֶׁר תֹּאמַר יִנָּתֵן לָהּ לָבוֹא עִמָּהּ מִבֵּית הַנָּשִׁים עַד־בֵּית הַמֶּלֶךְ: יד בָּעֶרֶב הִיא בָאָה וּבַבֹּקֶר הִיא שָׁבָה אֶל־בֵּית הַנָּשִׁים שֵׁנִי אֶל־יַד שַׁעֲשְׁגַז סְרִיס הַמֶּלֶךְ שֹׁמֵר הַפִּילַגְשִׁים לֹא־תָבוֹא עוֹד אֶל־הַמֶּלֶךְ כִּי אִם־חָפֵץ בָּהּ הַמֶּלֶךְ וְנִקְרְאָה בְשֵׁם: טו וּבְהַגִּיעַ תֹּר־אֶסְתֵּר בַּת־אֲבִיחַיִל דֹּד מָרְדֳּכַי אֲשֶׁר לָקַח־לוֹ לְבַת לָבוֹא אֶל־הַמֶּלֶךְ לֹא בִקְשָׁה דָּבָר כִּי אִם אֶת־אֲשֶׁר יֹאמַר הֵגַי סְרִיס־הַמֶּלֶךְ שֹׁמֵר הַנָּשִׁים וַתְּהִי אֶסְתֵּר נֹשֵׂאת חֵן בְּעֵינֵי כָּל־רֹאֶיהָ:

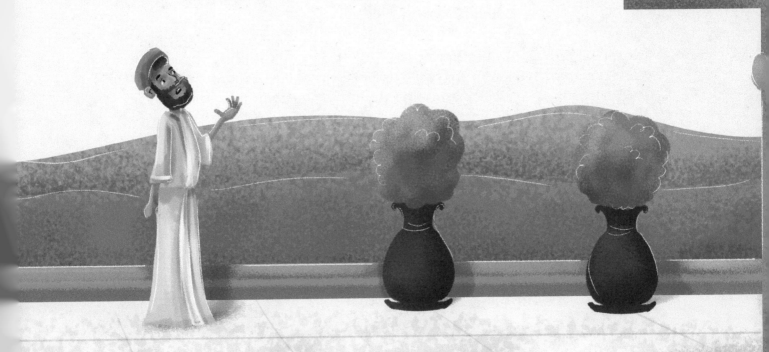

8 When the king's decree was obeyed, and when many young women were collected to Hegai's house in Shushan, Esther was also taken there. 9 She seemed good to Hegai, and he treated her kindly: he rushed to get her makeup and food and seven ladies-in-waiting from the king's palace. She and her maidens got more special treatment than anyone else. 10 Esther did not tell about her people or her origin, because Mordekhai instructed her not to tell. 11 Every day, Mordekhai would walk before the courtyard of the house where the women were kept to know how Esther was and what was happening to her. 12 As each woman's turn arrived to come to King Ahashverosh, each young woman spent a long time making herself look good–six months using oil of myrrh and six months using perfume and makeup– 13 whatever she asked for was given to her–and that's how she'd prepare to go to the king. 14 After that year, she would stay under the watch of Sha'ashgaz, and she would not come to the king again unless the king called her by name. 15 But when it was Esther's turn to go to the king–Esther, the daughter of Avihayil, uncle of Mordekhai, who had adopted her as a daughter–she did not ask for any special makeup, except for what Hegai instructed her. But everyone who saw her still admired her.

Pasuk 7
What was the relationship between Mordekhai and Esther?

According to Ralbag (France, 700 years ago), Esther 2:7 teaches us that they were first cousins. Esther's mother and her father, Avihayil, died when she was young, so Mordekhai looked after her as a foster father, and Esther was his בַּת (bat, daughter).

But R. Meir in the Gemara (Megillah 13a) tells us to read this word as בַּיִת (bayit). Bayit literally means "house," but it can also mean "wife." According to him, Mordekhai and Esther were actually married to each other! Rashi says this too. (Cousins don't get married very often, but it happens sometimes even today.)

• How does the story change depending on what relationship Mordekhai and Esther had? How would it affect their feelings when Ahashverosh took Esther away?

טז וַתִּלָּקַח אֶסְתֵּר אֶל־הַמֶּלֶךְ אֲחַשְׁוֵרוֹשׁ אֶל־בֵּית מַלְכוּתוֹ בַּחֹדֶשׁ הָעֲשִׂירִי הוּא־חֹדֶשׁ טֵבֵת בִּשְׁנַת־שֶׁבַע לְמַלְכוּתוֹ: יז וַיֶּאֱהַב הַמֶּלֶךְ אֶת־אֶסְתֵּר מִכָּל־הַנָּשִׁים

פסוק י"ז - PASUK 17
This pasuk is read in a special tune.

וַתִּשָּׂא־חֵן וָחֶסֶד לְפָנָיו מִכָּל־הַבְּתוּלוֹת וַיָּשֶׂם כֶּתֶר־מַלְכוּת בְּרֹאשָׁהּ וַיַּמְלִיכֶהָ תַּחַת וַשְׁתִּי: יח וַיַּעַשׂ הַמֶּלֶךְ מִשְׁתֶּה גָדוֹל לְכָל־שָׂרָיו וַעֲבָדָיו אֵת מִשְׁתֵּה אֶסְתֵּר וַהֲנָחָה לַמְּדִינוֹת עָשָׂה וַיִּתֵּן מַשְׂאֵת כְּיַד הַמֶּלֶךְ: יט וּבְהִקָּבֵץ בְּתוּלוֹת שֵׁנִית וּמָרְדֳּכַי יֹשֵׁב בְּשַׁעַר־הַמֶּלֶךְ: כ אֵין אֶסְתֵּר מַגֶּדֶת מוֹלַדְתָּהּ וְאֶת־עַמָּהּ כַּאֲשֶׁר צִוָּה עָלֶיהָ מָרְדֳּכָי וְאֶת־מַאֲמַר מָרְדֳּכַי אֶסְתֵּר עֹשָׂה כַּאֲשֶׁר הָיְתָה בְאָמְנָה אִתּוֹ: כא בַּיָּמִים הָהֵם וּמָרְדֳּכַי יוֹשֵׁב בְּשַׁעַר־הַמֶּלֶךְ קָצַף בִּגְתָן וָתֶרֶשׁ שְׁנֵי־סָרִיסֵי הַמֶּלֶךְ מִשֹּׁמְרֵי הַסַּף וַיְבַקְשׁוּ לִשְׁלֹחַ יָד בַּמֶּלֶךְ אֲחַשְׁוֵרֹשׁ: כב וַיִּוָּדַע הַדָּבָר לְמָרְדֳּכַי וַיַּגֵּד לְאֶסְתֵּר הַמַּלְכָּה וַתֹּאמֶר אֶסְתֵּר לַמֶּלֶךְ בְּשֵׁם מָרְדֳּכָי: כג וַיְבֻקַּשׁ הַדָּבָר וַיִּמָּצֵא וַיִּתָּלוּ שְׁנֵיהֶם עַל־עֵץ וַיִּכָּתֵב בְּסֵפֶר דִּבְרֵי הַיָּמִים לִפְנֵי הַמֶּלֶךְ:

16 Esther was taken to King Ahashverosh's palace in the tenth month, the month of Tevet, in the seventh year of his reign. 17 The king loved Esther more than all the other women, and she got his admiration and affection, and he put the royal crown on her head and made her queen instead of Vashti! 18 The king made a great banquet for all his nobles and servants—the Banquet of Esther. He also gave the provinces a tax break and gave gifts as he pleased. 19 When Ahashverosh collected women another time, Mordekhai was in the king's court. 20 Esther didn't tell her origin or her people, as Mordekhai instructed her, and she listened to Mordekhai just as she had when she was with him. 21 In those days, when Mordekhai was in the king's court, Bigtan and Teresh, two of the king's servants, got angry and plotted to kill King Ahashverosh. 22 Mordekhai found out and told Queen Esther, and Esther told the king, giving credit to Mordekhai. 23 It was investigated and found to be true, and the two of them were hanged on a wooden post. This was all written down in the King's Book of Chronicles.

CHAPTER 3 פֶּרֶק ג

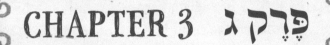

הַדְּבָרִים הָאֵלֶּה גִּדַּל הַמֶּלֶךְ אֲחַשְׁוֵרוֹשׁ אֶת־הָמָן בֶּן־הַמְּדָתָא הָאֲגָגִי וַיְנַשְּׂאֵהוּ וַיָּשֶׂם אֶת־כִּסְאוֹ מֵעַל כָּל־הַשָּׂרִים אֲשֶׁר אִתּוֹ: ב וְכָל־עַבְדֵי הַמֶּלֶךְ אֲשֶׁר־בְּשַׁעַר הַמֶּלֶךְ כֹּרְעִים וּמִשְׁתַּחֲוִים לְהָמָן כִּי־כֵן צִוָּה־לוֹ הַמֶּלֶךְ וּמָרְדֳּכַי לֹא יִכְרַע וְלֹא יִשְׁתַּחֲוֶה: ג וַיֹּאמְרוּ עַבְדֵי הַמֶּלֶךְ אֲשֶׁר־בְּשַׁעַר הַמֶּלֶךְ לְמָרְדֳּכָי מַדּוּעַ אַתָּה עוֹבֵר אֶת מִצְוַת הַמֶּלֶךְ:

1 After all this, King Ahashverosh promoted Haman son of Hammedata the Agagi and made him the highest-ranking noble. 2 All the servants in the king's court would bow to Haman because the king commanded it. But Mordekhai would not bow. 3 The servants in the king's court said to Mordekhai, "Why are you disobeying the king's command?"

שְׁאֵלוֹת
?
Scavenger Hunt

FIND THE ANSWERS IN CHAPTER 3!

1. How much money did Haman offer to Ahashverosh?

2. What did Ahashverosh give to Haman?

3. What mouthful of words describes the governors of Ahashverosh's provinces?

4. Listen in shul! Which pasuk contains words that are (often) read with the sad tune used for Megillat Eikhah?

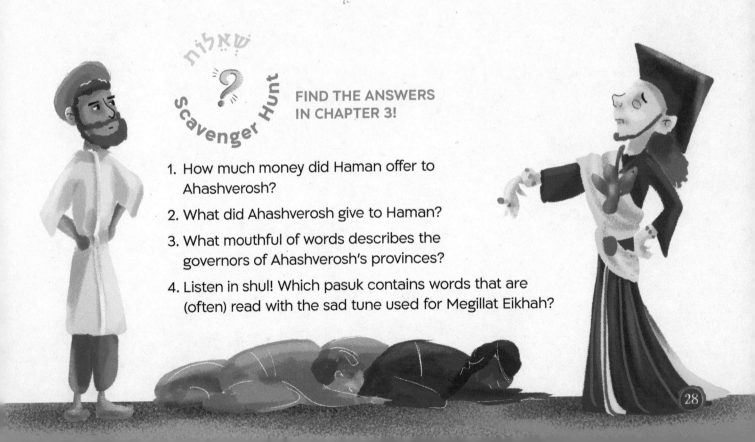

Pasuk 2
Mordekhai refuses to bow
to Haman—but why?

Ibn Ezra (Spain, 900 years ago)   אבן עזרא

On Haman's clothes was the image of an idol.

שֶׁהָיָה בְּבִגְדֵי הָמָן צוּרַת צַלְמֵי אֱלִיל.

Ibn Ezra's explanation—that Mordekhai refused to bow to Haman because it would have also meant bowing to an actual idol—appears in midrashim as well (like in Esther Rabbah 7:5).

- What's so wrong with bowing down to an idol?

- If Haman was attaching idols to himself, what can that tell us about how he viewed himself?

- You are never allowed to bow down to an idol, even if you don't believe in it and don't really think it's like God (Sefer HaHinukh, 28). Why do you think that is? Why would "faking it" not be allowed?

R. Yosef Kara (France, 900 years ago)   ר' יוסף קרא

I am a Jew, and I am not allowed to bow down to anyone except for God.

יְהוּדִי אָנֹכִי וְאֵינִי רַשַּׁאי לְהִשְׁתַּחֲוֹת וְלִכְרֹעַ כִּי אִם לַה' לְבַדּוֹ.

R. Kara suggests that Mordekhai's main reason for not bowing down wasn't just about an idol on Haman. It was more than that. Mordekhai believed Jews shouldn't bow to anyone or anything except God because that would go against what it means to be a Jew.

- What words in 3:4 could be evidence for R. Kara? How does he interpret those words?

Turn the page to read a story from the midrash that can help us understand R. Kara's interpretation.

« CONTINUED ON PAGE 31

ד וַיְהִי כְּאָמְרָם אֵלָיו יוֹם וָיוֹם וְלֹא שָׁמַע אֲלֵיהֶם וַיַּגִּידוּ לְהָמָן לִרְאוֹת הֲיַעַמְדוּ דִּבְרֵי מָרְדֳּכַי כִּי־הִגִּיד לָהֶם אֲשֶׁר־הוּא יְהוּדִי:

4 They would say this to him every day, but he didn't listen to them. They told this to Haman in order to see if Mordekhai would get away with it—for Mordekhai had told them that he was Jewish.

CONTINUED FROM PAGE 29 >>

Targum Sheni

תרגום שני אסתר ג:ג

מָן אִיתוֹי בַּר נָשָׁא דְּהוּא מִתְגָּאֶה וּמִתְרַבְרַב הוּא יְלוּד מִן אַנְתְּתָא וְיוֹמוֹי זְעִירִין... וְסוֹפֵיה חֲזֵיר לְעַפְרָא וַאֲנָא אִסְגּוּד קֳדָמוֹי? לָא אֲנָא סָגֵיד אֶלָּא לַא-לָהָא חַיָּיא וְקַיָּימָא....

עֲנַיִין וַאֲמַרִין לְמָרְדְּכַי: וְהָא אַשְׁכְּחָן דְּאַבְהָתָךְ סָגְדִין קֳדָם אֲבָהָתֵיה דְּהָמָן.

עֲנֵי מָרְדְּכַי וַאֲמַר לְהוֹן: מָן אִיתוֹי דְּסָגְדִין קֳדָם אֲבָהָתֵיה דְּהָמָן.

אַמְרִין לֵיהּ: לָא בְּרַע אֲבוּךְ יַעֲקֹב קֳדָם עֵשָׂו אֲחוּי דְּהוּא אֲבוּי דְּהָמָן.

אֲמַר לְהוֹן: אֲנָא מִן זַרְעִיתֵיה דְּבִנְיָמִין וְכַד סְגֵיד יַעֲקֹב קֳדָם עֵשָׂו בִּנְיָמִין לָא יְלוּד הֲוָה וְלָא סְגֵד קֳדָם אִינַשׁ מִן יוֹמוֹי. מְטוּל כְּדֵין נְטַר יָתֵיה קַיָּים עָלְמַיָּא בִּמְעֵי אִימֵּיהּ עַד עִידָּן דְּיִסְקוּן לְאַרְעָא דְּיִשְׂרָאֵל וְיֶהֱוֵי בֵּית מַקְדְּשָׁא בְּאַרְעֵיהּ.

Mordekhai thought: "Who is the person who is so proud and haughty, who is born from a woman, and whose days are so few… and whose ultimate end is a return to dust… shall I bow before such a person? I only bow down to the Eternal God…."

The people there said to Mordekhai: But we find that your ancestors bowed down before Haman's ancestors.

Mordekhai answered: Who was it that bowed down before Haman's ancestors?

They said to him: Didn't your ancestor Yaakov bow down before his brother Esav, who was Haman's ancestor?

Mordekhai: I am descended from Binyamin. When Yaakov bowed down before Esav, Binyamin was not yet born. So Binyamin never bowed before any human all his days. For this reason, the Eternal One of the World guarded him in his mother's womb, until the time that the Jewish people would go up to Eretz Yisrael and the Beit HaMikdash would be built in Binyamin's land.

- Why might Yaakov have thought it was okay to bow to someone? (Look it up! Bereishit 33:3.)

- According to this midrash, what was motivating Mordekhai to not bow? What would bowing to Haman represent?

- In this midrash, Mordekhai seems to be saying that his tradition from Binyamin is that he doesn't bow down to anyone, even if others (like Yaakov) might! How does that explain why the land of Binyamin is chosen as the perfect place for the Beit HaMikdash to be built?

- Can you imagine being forced to take an action (even if it's not idolatry) that contradicts your faith in God or your practice as a Jew? How would that feel? How would you react?

ה וַיַּרְא הָמָן כִּי־אֵין מָרְדֳּכַי כֹּרֵעַ וּמִשְׁתַּחֲוֶה לוֹ וַיִּמָּלֵא הָמָן חֵמָה: ו וַיִּבֶז בְּעֵינָיו לִשְׁלֹחַ יָד בְּמָרְדֳּכַי לְבַדּוֹ כִּי־הִגִּידוּ לוֹ אֶת־עַם מָרְדֳּכָי וַיְבַקֵּשׁ הָמָן לְהַשְׁמִיד אֶת־כָּל־הַיְּהוּדִים אֲשֶׁר בְּכָל־מַלְכוּת אֲחַשְׁוֵרוֹשׁ עַם מָרְדֳּכָי: ז בַּחֹדֶשׁ הָרִאשׁוֹן הוּא־חֹדֶשׁ נִיסָן בִּשְׁנַת שְׁתֵּים עֶשְׂרֵה לַמֶּלֶךְ אֲחַשְׁוֵרוֹשׁ הִפִּיל פּוּר הוּא הַגּוֹרָל לִפְנֵי הָמָן מִיּוֹם לְיוֹם וּמֵחֹדֶשׁ לְחֹדֶשׁ שְׁנֵים־עָשָׂר הוּא־חֹדֶשׁ אֲדָר: ח וַיֹּאמֶר הָמָן לַמֶּלֶךְ אֲחַשְׁוֵרוֹשׁ יֶשְׁנוֹ עַם־אֶחָד מְפֻזָּר וּמְפֹרָד בֵּין הָעַמִּים בְּכֹל מְדִינוֹת מַלְכוּתֶךָ וְדָתֵיהֶם שֹׁנוֹת מִכָּל־עָם וְאֶת־דָּתֵי הַמֶּלֶךְ אֵינָם עֹשִׂים וְלַמֶּלֶךְ אֵין־שֹׁוֶה לְהַנִּיחָם:

5 Haman saw that Mordekhai wouldn't bow to him, and Haman was filled with rage. 6 He had been told that Mordekhai was Jewish, so he didn't think it was enough to just kill Mordekhai. He wanted to destroy all the Jews in Ahashverosh's kingdom—all of Mordekhai's nation. 7 It was Nisan, the first month of the year, during the 12th year of King Ahashverosh's reign. Haman asked someone to make a *pur*—a kind of raffle—to pick the month and the day for destroying the Jews. It landed on Adar. 8 Haman said to King Ahashverosh, "In all the provinces of your kingdom, there's one nation that is scattered and separate. Their laws are different from all other nations, and they don't follow the king's laws. It's not worth it for Your Majesty to let them be.

2 According to R. Yeshayahu Horowitz, it's not that the Jews were separate from the rest of Ahashverosh's kingdom; it's that they were separate from each other:

R. Yeshayahu Horowitz (Prague, 450 years ago)

שני לוחות הברית, תצוה

Haman said that the Jewish people were divided, not unified, and spread all around. He noticed that even in their communities there

אָמַר הָמָן שֶׁהֵם בְּמַחֲלֹקֶת וְאֵינָם בְּאַחְדוּת אַחַת שֶׁהֲרֵי הֵם מְפֻזָּרִים בְּאַרְבַּע כַּנְפוֹת הָאָרֶץ, וְאַף בְּכָל קִבּוּץ וְקִבּוּץ מֵהֶם יֵשׁ פֵּרוּד וְעַל כֵּן יָכוֹל נוּכַל לָהֶם. וְכִרְאוֹת אֶסְתֵּר זֶה הַחֵטְא בְּיִשְׂרָאֵל... עַל כֵּן תִּקְּנָה זֶה וְאָמְרָה "לֵךְ כְּנוֹס."

was separation between them, and that's why he thought they could be beaten. When Esther saw this sin... she corrected it by saying, "Go gather together all the Jews" (4:16).

According to this interpretation, Haman understood that God would be upset about the Jewish people not being united, and this gave him an opportunity to attack them.

• Why is it so important to have unity?

• How does Esther's command to "gather together" the Jews solve the problem of not being united? What does R. Horowitz think Esther was asking the Jewish people to do?

• The word for "unity" in Hebrew is אַחְדוּת (ahdut), which literally means treating each other like brothers and sisters. Why does it make sense for Jewish people to treat each other that way?

פְּשָׁט

Reading the Verses

Pasuk 6

• What's unfair and cruel about Haman's behavior?

• Is it okay to judge and punish a whole group based on the actions of one individual?

פֵּרוּשׁ

Commentary

Pasuk 8
What did Haman mean when he described the Jewish people as "scattered and separate"? What had he noticed about the Jewish people, and what was he trying to express to Ahashverosh?

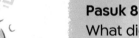

Here are two different ways to understand Haman's claim.

1 The Gemara (Megillah 13b) says that Haman observed how certain Jewish practices kept the Jewish people separate from people who weren't Jewish. For example, they refused to eat food from non-Jewish people (because of keeping kosher). The Gemara also says that Haman accused the Jewish people of being lazy because they refused to work on Shabbat and Yom Tov.

He was using their religious observances to exaggerate a story about how Jews don't help or work hard.

Mitzvot certainly do make the Jewish people different from others. But is being different a good reason to create fear or hatred of someone or to want to hurt them? Absolutely not!

• How would you respond to someone who felt confused or excluded by another person's unique practices? How should you treat other people when it comes to their religious practices, and how would you want them to treat you?

ט אִם־עַל־הַמֶּלֶךְ טוֹב יִכָּתֵב לְאַבְּדָם וַעֲשֶׂרֶת אֲלָפִים כִּכַּר־כֶּסֶף אֶשְׁקוֹל עַל־יְדֵי עֹשֵׂי הַמְּלָאכָה לְהָבִיא אֶל־גִּנְזֵי הַמֶּלֶךְ:

9 "If it pleases Your Majesty, let a decree be written to destroy them. I'll weigh out 10,000 talents of silver for your treasure vault."

Midrash

Pasuk 9
Haman tries to bribe Ahashverosh with "10,000 talents of silver" to let him kill the Jews. Why this specific number?

Rabbeinu Bahaye brings an idea from a midrash:

Rabbeinu Bahaye (Spain, 700 years ago)

ר' בחיי שמות לח:כה

כִּי מִפְּנֵי שֶׁיָּדַע הָמָן חֵטְא שִׁבְטֵי יִשְׂרָאֵל בִּמְכִירַת יוֹסֵף בְּעֶשְׂרִים כֶּסֶף שֶׁהֵם חֲמֵשֶׁת שְׁקָלִים וְעָנַשׁ הַחֵטְא הַהוּא לֹא נִפְקַד עֲלֵיהֶם עֲדַיִן עַל כֵּן חָשַׁב מַחֲשָׁבָה לִקְנוֹת כָּל יִשְׂרָאֵל לָתֵת בִּשְׁבִיל כָּל אֶחָד מִשִּׁשִּׁים רִבּוֹא חֲמֵשֶׁת שְׁקָלִים.... וּבְעִנְיָן שֶׁאָמְרוּ בַּמִּדְרָשׁ "וַיֵּשְׁבוּ לֶאֱכָל לֶחֶם" (בראשית לז:כה)—אָמַר לָהֶם הַקָּדוֹשׁ בָּרוּךְ הוּא אַתֶּם מְכַרְתֶּם אֶת אֲחִיכֶם מִתּוֹךְ מִשְׁתֶּה חַיֵּיכֶם שֶׁבְּנֵיכֶם נִמְכָּרִים בְּשׁוּשָׁן מִתּוֹךְ מִשְׁתֶּה שֶׁנֶּאֱמַר "וְהַמֶּלֶךְ וְהָמָן יָשְׁבוּ לִשְׁתּוֹת" (אסתר ג:טו).

Haman knew that the tribes of Israel sold Yosef for 20 silver coins, equaling 5 shekalim, and that they were never punished for this sin. So he figured he would use the same calculation to pay for every Jew: 5 shekalim per Jew for all 600,000 of them. This came to 10,000 talents of silver.... The connection to Yosef is recorded in the midrash as well, which states: "And they sat to eat bread (just before selling Yosef)" (Bereishit 37:25)—God said, "Just as you sold your brother through a banquet, I swear that your descendants will be sold in Shushan through a banquet." As it says, "The king and Haman sat down to have a drink" (Esther 3:15).

According to this explanation, Haman understood that Yosef's brothers—the שְׁבָטִים (shevatim, tribes), representing the whole Jewish people—should be held responsible for selling Yosef into slavery. So Haman thought that he could use that as his opportunity for destroying them. That's why he offered to "pay" for every Jew with the same price Yosef was sold for.

R. Bahaye studied kabbalah, which uses the number 600,000 to symbolize the grand total of all Jews (no matter how many there really are).

- **LOOK IT UP!** What's the connection between the Purim story and the sale of Yosef in Bereishit 37? (See page 69 for more connections between Yosef and Megillat Esther!)

- The midrash also sees a connection between these stories because the shevatim sat down to eat and drink just before selling Yosef (and right after throwing him in a pit), the same way Ahashverosh and Haman sit to eat and drink after deciding to kill the Jewish people. What's shocking about that behavior? What does eating and drinking as if everything is just fine tell us about their attitude toward the people who would suffer, like Yosef in Bereishit or the Jewish people in Esther?

י וַיָּסַר הַמֶּלֶךְ אֶת־טַבַּעְתּוֹ מֵעַל יָדוֹ וַיִּתְּנָהּ לְהָמָן בֶּן־הַמְּדָתָא הָאֲגָגִי צֹרֵר הַיְּהוּדִים: יא וַיֹּאמֶר
הַמֶּלֶךְ לְהָמָן הַכֶּסֶף נָתוּן לָךְ וְהָעָם לַעֲשׂוֹת בּוֹ כַּטּוֹב בְּעֵינֶיךָ: יב וַיִּקָּרְאוּ סֹפְרֵי הַמֶּלֶךְ בַּחֹדֶשׁ
הָרִאשׁוֹן בִּשְׁלוֹשָׁה עָשָׂר יוֹם בּוֹ וַיִּכָּתֵב כְּכָל־אֲשֶׁר־צִוָּה הָמָן אֶל אֲחַשְׁדַּרְפְּנֵי־הַמֶּלֶךְ וְאֶל־
הַפַּחוֹת אֲשֶׁר עַל־מְדִינָה וּמְדִינָה וְאֶל־שָׂרֵי עַם וָעָם מְדִינָה וּמְדִינָה כִּכְתָבָהּ וְעַם וָעָם כִּלְשׁוֹנוֹ
בְּשֵׁם הַמֶּלֶךְ אֲחַשְׁוֵרֹשׁ נִכְתָּב וְנֶחְתָּם בְּטַבַּעַת הַמֶּלֶךְ: יג וְנִשְׁלוֹחַ סְפָרִים בְּיַד הָרָצִים אֶל־כָּל־
מְדִינוֹת הַמֶּלֶךְ לְהַשְׁמִיד לַהֲרֹג וּלְאַבֵּד אֶת־כָּל־הַיְּהוּדִים מִנַּעַר וְעַד־זָקֵן טַף וְנָשִׁים בְּיוֹם
אֶחָד בִּשְׁלוֹשָׁה עָשָׂר לְחֹדֶשׁ שְׁנֵים־עָשָׂר הוּא־חֹדֶשׁ אֲדָר וּשְׁלָלָם לָבוֹז: יד פַּתְשֶׁגֶן הַכְּתָב
לְהִנָּתֵן דָּת בְּכָל־מְדִינָה וּמְדִינָה גָּלוּי לְכָל־הָעַמִּים לִהְיוֹת עֲתִדִים
לַיּוֹם הַזֶּה: טו הָרָצִים יָצְאוּ דְחוּפִים בִּדְבַר הַמֶּלֶךְ וְהַדָּת נִתְּנָה בְּשׁוּשַׁן
הַבִּירָה וְהַמֶּלֶךְ וְהָמָן יָשְׁבוּ לִשְׁתּוֹת וְהָעִיר שׁוּשָׁן נָבוֹכָה:

PASUK 15 - פסוק ט"ו
The words וְהָעִיר שׁוּשָׁן נָבוֹכָה (but
the city of Shushan was in a state of
shock) are read in the sad tune of
Megillat Eikhah.

36

10 So the king removed his ring and gave it to Haman son of Hammedata the Agagi, enemy of the Jews. 11 The king said to Haman, "Keep your money. Do whatever you want with that nation." 12 The king's scribes were called on the 13th day of Nisan. Everything that Haman commanded to the ahashdarpenei ha-melekh (the king's highest officers) and governors was written and sent out to each and every province and people, in their own languages. It was written in King Ahashverosh's name and sealed with the king's ring. 13 Scrolls were sent with the messengers to all the king's provinces saying to destroy, murder, and annihilate all the Jews–from young to old, including children and women–on the 13th day of Adar. All the Jews' possessions would also be free for the taking. 14 The published decree was displayed in every province so that all the nations would be ready for this day. 15 The messengers were rushed out with the king's message. The law was proclaimed in Shushan. The king and Haman sat down to have a drink, but the city of Shushan was in a state of shock.

CHAPTER 4   פֶּרֶק ד

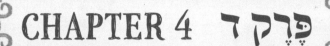

Pasuk 1 - א פסוק
This pasuk is read in the sad
tune of Megillat Eikhah.

וּמָרְדֳּכַי
א

יָדַע אֶת־כָּל־אֲשֶׁר נַעֲשָׂה וַיִּקְרַע מָרְדֳּכַי
אֶת־בְּגָדָיו וַיִּלְבַּשׁ שַׂק וָאֵפֶר וַיֵּצֵא בְּתוֹךְ
הָעִיר וַיִּזְעַק זְעָקָה גְדוֹלָה וּמָרָה: ב וַיָּבוֹא עַד לִפְנֵי שַׁעַר־הַמֶּלֶךְ
כִּי אֵין לָבוֹא אֶל־שַׁעַר הַמֶּלֶךְ בִּלְבוּשׁ שָׂק:

1 Mordekhai found out everything that had happened. He tore his clothes, dressed in rags, and put ashes on himself. He went out into the city and cried a great and bitter cry. 2 He went right up to the king's court, because it was not allowed to enter the king's court in rags.

שְׁאֵלוֹת
?
Scavenger Hunt

FIND THE ANSWERS IN CHAPTER 4!

1. What did Esther hear from her servants that made her very upset?

2. How long had it been since Ahashverosh last called Esther to come see him?

3. What does Mordekhai seem not to know?

4. How long did Esther ask Mordekhai and all of the Jews of Shushan to fast with her?

Pasuk 3 - ג פסוק
This pasuk is read in the sad
tune of Megillat Eikhah.

ג וּבְכָל־מְדִינָה וּמְדִינָה מְקוֹם אֲשֶׁר דְּבַר־הַמֶּלֶךְ וְדָתוֹ מַגִּיעַ אֵבֶל גָּדוֹל לַיְּהוּדִים וְצוֹם וּבְכִי וּמִסְפֵּד שַׂק וָאֵפֶר יֻצַּע לָרַבִּים: ד וַתָּבוֹאנָה נַעֲרוֹת אֶסְתֵּר וְסָרִיסֶיהָ וַיַּגִּידוּ לָהּ וַתִּתְחַלְחַל הַמַּלְכָּה מְאֹד וַתִּשְׁלַח בְּגָדִים לְהַלְבִּישׁ אֶת־מָרְדֳּכַי וּלְהָסִיר שַׂקּוֹ מֵעָלָיו וְלֹא קִבֵּל: ה וַתִּקְרָא אֶסְתֵּר לַהֲתָךְ מִסָּרִיסֵי הַמֶּלֶךְ אֲשֶׁר הֶעֱמִיד לְפָנֶיהָ וַתְּצַוֵּהוּ עַל־מָרְדֳּכָי לָדַעַת מַה־זֶּה וְעַל־מַה־זֶּה: ו וַיֵּצֵא הֲתָךְ אֶל־מָרְדֳּכָי אֶל־רְחוֹב הָעִיר אֲשֶׁר לִפְנֵי שַׁעַר־הַמֶּלֶךְ: ז וַיַּגֶּד־לוֹ מָרְדֳּכַי אֵת כָּל־אֲשֶׁר קָרָהוּ וְאֵת פָּרָשַׁת הַכֶּסֶף אֲשֶׁר אָמַר הָמָן לִשְׁקוֹל עַל־גִּנְזֵי הַמֶּלֶךְ בַּיְּהוּדִים לְאַבְּדָם: ח וְאֶת־פַּתְשֶׁגֶן כְּתָב־הַדָּת אֲשֶׁר־נִתַּן בְּשׁוּשָׁן לְהַשְׁמִידָם נָתַן לוֹ לְהַרְאוֹת אֶת־אֶסְתֵּר וּלְהַגִּיד לָהּ וּלְצַוּוֹת עָלֶיהָ לָבוֹא אֶל־הַמֶּלֶךְ לְהִתְחַנֶּן־לוֹ וּלְבַקֵּשׁ מִלְּפָנָיו עַל־עַמָּהּ: ט וַיָּבוֹא הֲתָךְ וַיַּגֵּד לְאֶסְתֵּר אֵת דִּבְרֵי מָרְדֳּכָי: י וַתֹּאמֶר אֶסְתֵּר לַהֲתָךְ וַתְּצַוֵּהוּ אֶל־מָרְדֳּכָי: יא כָּל־עַבְדֵי הַמֶּלֶךְ וְעַם מְדִינוֹת הַמֶּלֶךְ יֹדְעִים אֲשֶׁר כָּל־אִישׁ וְאִשָּׁה אֲשֶׁר־יָבוֹא אֶל־הַמֶּלֶךְ אֶל־הֶחָצֵר הַפְּנִימִית אֲשֶׁר לֹא־יִקָּרֵא אַחַת דָּתוֹ לְהָמִית לְבַד מֵאֲשֶׁר יוֹשִׁיט־לוֹ הַמֶּלֶךְ אֶת־שַׁרְבִיט הַזָּהָב וְחָיָה וַאֲנִי לֹא נִקְרֵאתִי לָבוֹא אֶל־הַמֶּלֶךְ זֶה שְׁלוֹשִׁים יוֹם: יב וַיַּגִּידוּ לְמָרְדֳּכָי אֵת דִּבְרֵי אֶסְתֵּר:

3 In every province, wherever the king's law reached, there was great mourning among the Jews. They fasted, cried, and grieved. Everyone put on rags. 4 Esther's servants came and told her about Mordekhai's behavior, and she was very disturbed. She sent clothes for Mordekhai to wear instead of his rags, but he wouldn't accept it. 5 Esther called her servant Hatakh and commanded him to figure out what exactly was going on with Mordekhai. 6 Hatakh went out and found Mordekhai in the city square right in front of the king's court. 7 Mordekhai told him about everything that happened, including the silver that Haman said he would measure out from the king's vault in order to annihilate the Jews. 8 Mordekhai gave Hatakh the published decree that had been posted in Shushan to show it to Esther. Mordekhai sent Hatakh back to command Esther to go to the king and beg for her people. 9 Hatakh came back and told Esther what Mordekhai said. 10 Esther told Hatakh to go command Mordekhai: 11 "Everyone in the kingdom knows that anyone who enters the king's inner chamber without being summoned shares the same verdict: death! The only exception is if the king extends his golden scepter. And I have not been summoned to the king for 30 days." 12 They told Mordekhai what Esther said.

Megillah Trop

Most of the time, Megillat Esther is chanted in a tune that sounds happy and lighthearted. But sometimes, the reading slips into a sad and mournful tune, like for pesukim 1 and 3.

When these words are read in shul, the custom is to switch out of the tune for Megillat Esther, and instead use the tune for Megillat Eikhah, which is what we read on Tisha B'Av (when we mourn the destruction of the Beit HaMikdash). Why do we change back and forth like this?

The story of Esther has a lot of connections to the destruction of the Beit HaMikdash. Mordekhai and many other Jews were exiled as part of that destruction (see Esther 2:6), and that's how they ended up in Ahashverosh's kingdom.

But also, the story in Megillat Esther was so close to being an Eikhah story. We now know that the Purim story ended well, and we celebrate it with great joy. But Mordekhai and Esther and the Jews of Shushan and Persia didn't know that. For them, in the middle of the story, they were afraid it could still turn out to be a national tragedy or even the end of our people altogether. This caused them real suffering, and it causes us suffering, too, when we think of their sorrow and remember what might have happened.

Remembering how close Haman came to destroying all of us also helps us fully appreciate God's miracles and celebrate the joy of being saved!

יג וַיֹּאמֶר מָרְדֳּכַי לְהָשִׁיב אֶל־אֶסְתֵּר אַל־תְּדַמִּי בְנַפְשֵׁךְ לְהִמָּלֵט בֵּית־הַמֶּלֶךְ מִכָּל־הַיְּהוּדִים: יד כִּי אִם־הַחֲרֵשׁ תַּחֲרִישִׁי בָּעֵת הַזֹּאת רֶוַח וְהַצָּלָה יַעֲמוֹד לַיְּהוּדִים מִמָּקוֹם אַחֵר וְאַתְּ וּבֵית־אָבִיךְ תֹּאבֵדוּ וּמִי יוֹדֵעַ אִם־לְעֵת כָּזֹאת הִגַּעַתְּ לַמַּלְכוּת:

13 Mordekhai sent this message back to Esther: "Don't imagine that you alone of all the Jews will be saved in the king's palace. 14 If you keep silent now, the Jews will be saved another way, and you and your family will be lost. And who knows if you became queen for this very moment?"

God is not mentioned anywhere in the Megillah! (See page 55.) But Ralbag thinks Mordekhai is talking about God in this pasuk and is sharing with Esther that he wonders whether God helped her become queen for exactly this reason: to be the only person who could save the Jewish people when they needed it most!

• It must have been difficult for the Jewish people in the story to not know whether they would be saved or not. In some ways, their experience of God is similar to our own. We don't have prophets, so we don't know what God is thinking or doing. Still, is it sometimes possible to feel like God is involved in our lives and stories? How?

• Could both Malbim and Ralbag be correct? How?

Pasuk 14
What does Mordekhai mean when he says, "Who knows if you became queen for this very moment?"

Malbim (Eastern Europe, 200 years ago)   מלבי״ם

He means to say, "Don't think you can just save them later when you might be called by the king. It could be that God will only allow you to save them right now; today! And if you wait until tomorrow, your time will have passed."

רוֹצֶה לוֹמַר בַּל תַּחְשְׁבִי כִּי תִּהְיִי לָהֶם עֵזֶר לִתְשׁוּעָתָם אַחַר יָמִים אֲחָדִים, שֶׁתִּהְיִי קְרוּאָה מִן הַמֶּלֶךְ, כִּי יוּכַל לִהְיוֹת שֶׁאוֹתָךְ לֹא הִזְמִין ה׳ רַק לְעֵת הַזֹּאת שֶׁעַל יָדֵךְ תִּהְיֶה תְּשׁוּעָתָם הַיּוֹם, וְאִם תַּמְתִּינִי עַד לְמָחָר עָבַר זְמַנֵּךְ.

Esther faced a difficult choice. If she went to Ahashverosh without being called, he might kill her! But it would be almost a whole year until Haman put his evil decree into action, so perhaps she had time to wait and see if Ahashverosh would call her on his own. So should she wait a bit longer, hoping that he might do that? Or should she go right away? Malbim thinks Mordekhai is advising Esther not to wait even one day to act! This is called "seizing the moment."

- In the end, Esther did act right away. Where did she find the courage to do what she did? What do you think you would have done?

- Why is it important to seize the moment when you have an opportunity to do something good? What could happen if you push it off until later?

Ralbag (France, 700 years ago)   רלב״ג

He means to say, "Who knows if you became a ruler for exactly this kind of moment, which is a time of trouble for Israel? Perhaps God arranged this as a way of watching over Israel in order for them to be saved by your hands!"

רוֹצֶה לוֹמַר וּמִי יוֹדֵעַ אִם בַּעֲבוּר עֵת כָּזֹאת שֶׁהוּא עֵת רָעָה לְיִשְׂרָאֵל הִגַּעַתְּ לַמַּלְכוּת כְּדֵי שֶׁתַּגִּיעַ לָהֶם הַהַצָּלָה עַל יָדֵךְ וְסִבֵּב הַשֵּׁם יִתְבָּרַךְ זֶה לְהַשְׁגָּחָה עַל יִשְׂרָאֵל.

טו וַתֹּאמֶר אֶסְתֵּר לְהָשִׁיב אֶל־מָרְדֳּכָי: טז לֵךְ כְּנוֹס אֶת־כָּל־הַיְּהוּדִים הַנִּמְצְאִים בְּשׁוּשָׁן וְצוּמוּ
עָלַי וְאַל־תֹּאכְלוּ וְאַל־תִּשְׁתּוּ שְׁלֹשֶׁת יָמִים לַיְלָה וָיוֹם גַּם־אֲנִי וְנַעֲרֹתַי אָצוּם כֵּן ...

15 Esther sent this message back to Mordekhai: 16 "Go gather together all the Jews of Shushan and
fast for me. Don't eat or drink for three whole days. My servants and I will also fast.

44

תְּפִלָּה

Tefillah

Pasuk 16
What can we learn from Esther's words
לֵךְ כְּנוֹס (lekh kenos, go gather together)?

Maharal (Prague, 500 years ago)

אור חדש למהר"ל

This hinted to Mordekhai about prayer, telling him that all the Jews should pray. The words "go gather together" meant that they should gather in shul

דָּבָר זֶה רָמְזָה לוֹ עַל הַתְּפִלָּה, שֶׁיִּתְפַּלְלוּ, וּבְדָבָר זֶה שֶׁיָּךְ "לֵךְ כְּנוֹס"—כַּאֲשֶׁר יֵלְכוּ לְבֵית הַכְּנֶסֶת לְהִתְפַּלֵּל, וְלֹא יִתְפַּלֵּל כָּל אֶחָד בְּבֵיתוֹ, רַק תִּהְיֶה תְּפִלַּת צִבּוּר.

to pray and that they shouldn't pray by themselves in their houses. Rather, it should be communal prayer.

The Hebrew term for shul is בֵּית כְּנֶסֶת (beit keneset). This literally means "a house of gathering together." Maharal suggests that when Esther told Mordekhai to "gather" the Jews, it meant more than just being in one place together. It meant praying together!

Back in chapter 3, we saw a comment from R. Yeshayahu Horowitz about how Haman saw that the Jewish people were split into different groups, and Esther tried to fix that problem (page 32). According to Maharal, gathering together wouldn't just be a way to solve their disunity, but would also be the way they should pray.

- Why would a shul be called a beit keneset? In what ways are gathering and praying connected to each other?

- How does praying together with your community feel different from praying alone? What are examples of circumstances when you'd rather do one or the other?

- In what ways can it be helpful to pray as a community when times are hard?

פסוק ט"ז - PASUK 16
(And וְכַאֲשֶׁר אָבַדְתִּי) The words
if I die, then so be it) are read in the
sad tune of Megillat Eikhah.

... וּבְכֵן אָבוֹא אֶל־הַמֶּלֶךְ אֲשֶׁר לֹא־כַדָּת וְכַאֲשֶׁר אָבַדְתִּי אָבָדְתִּי:

יז וַיַּעֲבֹר מָרְדֳּכָי וַיַּעַשׂ כְּכֹל אֲשֶׁר־צִוְּתָה עָלָיו אֶסְתֵּר:

"And so I will go to the king, breaking the law. And if I die, then so be it." 17 So Mordekhai went and did everything Esther commanded him.

Many rabbis agree that risking one's own life to save another person is a great mitzvah, but you don't **have** to do it (e.g., see Tzitz Eliezer 10:25, ch. 7).

- Why do you think halakhah wants us to sometimes look out for our own lives first? What is that supposed to teach us?

- What's an example of a time when people should risk (or even give up) their lives in order to save others? Why?

In the Sifra, one person might have to risk their life to save one other person. But Esther was trying to save the whole Jewish people. Many rabbis believe risking your life to save the whole people is more of an obligation and less of a choice (e.g., see Shevet Mi-Yehudah, page 83).

- Why do you think saving the whole people is different from saving one person? What do you think R. Akiva would say about Esther's situation?

הֲלָכָה
Halakhah

Pasuk 16
A midrash notices that Esther is doing something extremely heroic.

Targum Rishon

תרגום ראשון

I die from this world in order to save the people of the House of Israel.

אוֹבֵד מִן חַיֵּי עָלְמָא הָדֵין בְּגִין פּוּרְקַן עַמָּא בֵּית יִשְׂרָאֵל.

Esther seems to be saying that she knows there's a chance she might die, but she's willing to take that chance in order to try to save the Jews. She understands that her sacrifice might not pay off, but she is risking her life for the chance to save everyone.

That's not an easy choice to make. Is it correct to sacrifice yourself to save someone else?

It's a debate!

Sifra (Eretz Yisrael, 1,800 years ago)

ספרא בהר פרשה ה:ג

There were two people walking through the desert and only one of them had a jug of water. If one were to drink the whole thing, that person would be able to stay alive and make it through the desert to a town. But if they split the water, they would both die (because it wouldn't be enough to keep either person alive).

שְׁנַיִם שֶׁהָלְכוּ בַמִּדְבָּר, וְאֵין בְּיַד אֶחָד מֵהֶם אֶלָּא קִיתוֹן אֶחָד שֶׁל מַיִם. אִם שׁוֹתֵהוּ אֶחָד, מַגִּיעַ הוּא לַיִּשּׁוּב, וְאִם שׁוֹתִין אוֹתוֹ שְׁנַיִם, שְׁנֵיהֶם מֵתִים.

Ben Petori taught: They should both drink and die, because the Torah says, "Your brother shall live **with you**" (Vayikra 25:36).

דָּרַשׁ בֶּן פְּטוֹרִי: יִשְׁתּוּ שְׁנֵיהֶן וְיָמוּתוּ, שֶׁנֶּאֱמַר "וְחֵי אָחִיךָ **עִמָּךְ**" (ויקרא כה:לו).

R. Akiva replied: "Your brother **shall live** with you" means that you have to make sure you live before making sure someone else does.

אָמַר לוֹ רַבִּי עֲקִיבָה: "**וְחֵי אָחִיךָ** עִמָּךְ"—חַיֶּיךָ קוֹדְמִין לְחַיָּיו.

It's an intense situation, and we certainly hope to never encounter anything like this! Ben Petori seems to be focusing on עִמָּךְ (imakh, with you). He thinks the Torah is telling us: Live or die, you have to do it together because we have responsibility for each other. R. Akiva seems to be focusing on וְחֵי (ve-hei, shall live). He thinks the Torah is telling us: It's true we have responsibility for each other, but only if that leads to living in the end. If both people die, what good is that?

CHAPTER 5   פֶּרֶק ה

א וַיְהִי בַּיּוֹם הַשְּׁלִישִׁי וַתִּלְבַּשׁ אֶסְתֵּר מַלְכוּת וַתַּעֲמֹד בַּחֲצַר בֵּית־הַמֶּלֶךְ הַפְּנִימִית נֹכַח בֵּית הַמֶּלֶךְ וְהַמֶּלֶךְ יוֹשֵׁב עַל־כִּסֵּא מַלְכוּתוֹ בְּבֵית הַמַּלְכוּת נֹכַח פֶּתַח הַבָּיִת: ב וַיְהִי כִרְאוֹת הַמֶּלֶךְ אֶת־אֶסְתֵּר הַמַּלְכָּה עֹמֶדֶת בֶּחָצֵר נָשְׂאָה חֵן בְּעֵינָיו וַיּוֹשֶׁט הַמֶּלֶךְ לְאֶסְתֵּר אֶת־הַשַּׁרְבִיט הַזָּהָב אֲשֶׁר בְּיָדוֹ וַתִּקְרַב אֶסְתֵּר וַתִּגַּע בְּרֹאשׁ הַשַּׁרְבִיט:

1 It was the third day, and Esther dressed in her royal robes. She stood in the inner courtyard facing the palace, and the king sat on his throne facing the door. 2 When the king saw Queen Esther standing in the courtyard, she awakened compassion in him. The king extended the golden scepter in his hand, and Esther approached until she touched the tip of the scepter.

FIND THE ANSWERS IN CHAPTER 5!

1. What did Zeresh and all of Haman's friends tell him to do?

2. What was very tall, and how tall was it?

3. What did Esther ask Ahashverosh?

4. When was Mordekhai going to be hanged?

Pasuk 1

Esther goes to speak to Ahashverosh on the third day of her three-day fast. This seems like a long time to fast! Is there something Esther has in mind when she chooses that number of days?

Bereishit Rabbah 56:1

Our Rabbis said: It was in the merit of the third day of getting ready at Har Sinai, which is the day of matan Torah (the giving of the Torah), as it says, "On the **third day**, when it was morning..." (Shemot 19:16).

But R. Levi said: It was in the merit of the third day of Avraham, which was the day of עֲקֵדַת יִצְחָק (Akeidat Yitzhak, the sacrifice of Yitzhak), as it says, "On the **third day** (of traveling), he saw the place from afar" (Bereishit 22:4).

בראשית רבה נו:א

רַבָּנָן אָמְרֵי בִּזְכוּת יוֹם הַשְּׁלִישִׁי שֶׁל מַתַּן תּוֹרָה, שֶׁנֶּאֱמַר: וַיְהִי בַיּוֹם הַשְּׁלִישִׁי בִּהְיֹת הַבֹּקֶר.

וְרַבִּי לֵוִי אָמַר בִּזְכוּת שֶׁל יוֹם שְׁלִישִׁי שֶׁל אַבְרָהָם אָבִינוּ, שֶׁנֶּאֱמַר: בַּיּוֹם הַשְּׁלִישִׁי וַיַּרְא אֶת הַמָּקוֹם מֵרָחֹק.

According to this midrash, Esther's three-day fast was a kind of request to God. She was asking that a different great moment in Jewish history make the Jewish people worthy of being saved in her time. The Rabbis think that was receiving the Torah, and R. Levi thinks it was the Akeidah, because the Torah describes both of those stories as taking place "on the third day."

- A זְכוּת (zekhut, merit) is a kind of value or worth you can earn for doing something good in the past. Why do you think the merits from matan Torah or the Akeidah—which happened hundreds of years before the Purim story—would last so long?

- Can you think of other connections between the Purim story and matan Torah? (If you need some help, see page 89 and page 101.) Can you think of a connection to Akeidat Yitzhak?

- How might either one make the Jewish people worthy of being saved?

ג וַיֹּאמֶר לָהּ הַמֶּלֶךְ מַה־לָּךְ אֶסְתֵּר הַמַּלְכָּה וּמַה־בַּקָּשָׁתֵךְ עַד־חֲצִי הַמַּלְכוּת וְיִנָּתֵן לָךְ:
ד וַתֹּאמֶר אֶסְתֵּר אִם־עַל־הַמֶּלֶךְ טוֹב יָבוֹא הַמֶּלֶךְ וְהָמָן הַיּוֹם אֶל־הַמִּשְׁתֶּה אֲשֶׁר־עָשִׂיתִי לוֹ:

3 The king said to her, "How are you, Queen Esther? And what's your request? You can ask for up to half the kingdom and it will be given to you!" 4 Esther said, "If it please Your Majesty, may the king and Haman come today to a banquet I have made for him."

Pasuk 3

- Do you think Ahashverosh sounds serious, or is he exaggerating? Based on what you know about Ahashverosh's behavior in the rest of the Megillah, what's the most reasonable way to interpret his words and imagine his tone?

- How do you think Esther seems to be feeling after he says this to her?

Pasuk 4
There's something special about Esther's words.

Rabbeinu Bahaye (Spain, 700 years ago)	**כד הקמח, פורים**
There's a code in the first letters of יָבֹא הַמֶּלֶךְ וְהָמָן הַיּוֹם (may the king and Haman come today). They spell God's name!	"יָבֹא הַמֶּלֶךְ וְהָמָן הַיּוֹם"—בְּכָאן נִרְשַׁם הַשֵּׁם הַמְּיֻחָד בְּרֶמֶז.

There might be more hints to God's name in the Megillah other than this! Check out page 42!

In the introduction to his commentary on Megillat Esther, Ibn Ezra comments on something unusual: God's name does not appear anywhere in the Megillah, even though it's one of the holy books of Tanakh.

- Isn't that odd? If a book is part of the Bible, shouldn't it have to do with God somehow?!

- If God's name isn't in the Megillah, why is this book in the Tanakh at all? (Look at page 103.)

- **CHALLENGE!** As you read through the Megillah, try seeing if you can find God's name. We bet you won't!

- According to Maharal, what big part of the story is "hidden" (besides God's name)? How does hiding God's name in the story match the kind of miracles the Jews experienced in it?

- An open miracle is obvious, like the oil for the menorah lasting for eight nights instead of one. But a hidden miracle is more natural, like Esther becoming queen or Mordekhai being in the right place to save the king's life. Those kinds of things can still be miracles, but they're harder to notice. If you experienced a hidden miracle, what makes it challenging to see God behind it? Based on this, what might the Jews in the Purim story have been feeling?

- In times of hester panim, God is not gone, but God is more hidden from the Jewish people. When a person hides their face, you feel less connected to them. And that's what it's like with God when there's hester panim. Why would hidden miracles be the only kinds you find in a time of hester panim? What do miracles during a time of hester panim show about God's love for the Jewish people?

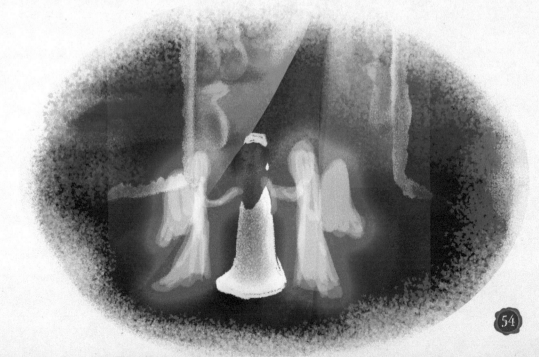

Tell Me More — נאמר נדבר על

> Why isn't God's name written in the story? Wasn't it a miracle that we were saved?

Here are two ideas from our פַּרְשָׁנִים (parshanim, commentators):

Rav Kohen Tzedek Gaon (Baghdad, 1,000 years ago)

Why isn't God's name written in the Megillah?... The Talmud states (Rosh Hashanah 18b) that people used to write God's name on their legal contracts and letters.... But the Sages said, "Later, when they pay their loans, they'll throw those documents in the garbage!" So they made a law not to do that, and that day became a holiday because of how important that law was! Here too, since Megillat Esther is called an "אִגֶּרֶת" (iggeret, letter)... they didn't want to write God's name in it.

תשובות הגאונים שערי תשובה סימן רא

לָמָּה לֹא נִכְתַּב שְׁמוֹ שֶׁל הַקָּדוֹשׁ בָּרוּךְ הוּא בִּמְגִלַּת אֶסְתֵּר?... כָּתוּב בְּמַסֶּכֶת רֹאשׁ הַשָּׁנָה הָיוּ רְגִילִים לִכְתֹּב אֶת הַשֵּׁם בְּאִגְרוֹת חוֹבוֹת.... וְאָמְרוּ חֲכָמִים לְמָחָר זֶה פּוֹרֵעַ אֶת חוֹבוֹ וְנִמְצָא הַשְּׁטָר מֻטָּל בָּאַשְׁפָּה. עָמְדוּ וּבִטְּלוּם וְאוֹתוֹ יוֹם עֲשָׂאוּהוּ יוֹם טוֹב, הָכִי נָמֵי כֵּיוָן דִמְגִלַּת אֶסְתֵּר נִקְרֵאת אִגֶּרֶת... לֹא רָצוּ לִכְתֹּב בָּהּ שֵׁם הַקָּדוֹשׁ בָּרוּךְ הוּא.

- The Megillah is called an iggeret twice in perek 9. Can you find both places?

- According to Rav Kohen Tzedek Gaon, what could have happened if God's name were written down in a document that wouldn't have been treated with respect? What can this teach us about writing, using, and respecting God's name in our own lives?

Maharal suggests a different reason for why God's name is not in the Megillah:

Maharal (Prague, 500 years ago)

She was called Esther because Israel were in a time of total hester panim (God's face being hidden), and that's why in this geulah (redemption) you won't find what can be found in all other examples of geulah. Even the miracle of Hanukkah was revealed through the lamps. But this geulah (in the Megillah) had no revealed miracle.... This is why the name of God isn't mentioned in the Megillah. But don't say that this makes the Purim geulah less important. The opposite is true! It's even greater for geulah to occur in a time of hester panim.

אור חדש למהר"ל אסתר ב:כב

וּלְכָךְ נִקְרֵאת אֶסְתֵּר עַל שֵׁם שֶׁהָיוּ יִשְׂרָאֵל בְּהֶסְתֵּר פָּנִים לְגַמְרֵי וּמִפְּנֵי כָּךְ לֹא תִּמְצָא בַּגְּאֻלָּה הַזֹּאת מַה שֶׁתִּמְצָא בִּשְׁאָר הַגְּאֻלּוֹת כִּי אַף נֵס חֲנֻכָּה הָיָה נִגְלָה בְּנֵרוֹת חֲנֻכָּה וְאֵלּוּ גְּאֻלָּה זֹאת לֹא הָיָה בָּהּ נֵס נִגְלֶה.... וּלְכָךְ לֹא נִזְכַּר הַשֵּׁם בַּמְּגִלָּה וְאַל תֹּאמַר כִּי בִּשְׁבִיל זֶה הַגְּאֻלָּה הַזֹּאת הִיא יוֹתֵר קְטַנָּה כִּי אַדְּרַבָּא כִּי דָבָר זֶה מוֹרֶה שֶׁהוּא יוֹתֵר גְּדוֹלָה מְאֹד לִגְאֹל אוֹתָם אַף כַּאֲשֶׁר הָיָה בְּהַסְתָּרַת פָּנִים.

ה וַיֹּאמֶר הַמֶּלֶךְ מַהֲרוּ אֶת־הָמָן לַעֲשׂוֹת אֶת־דְּבַר אֶסְתֵּר וַיָּבֹא הַמֶּלֶךְ וְהָמָן אֶל־הַמִּשְׁתֶּה אֲשֶׁר־עָשְׂתָה אֶסְתֵּר: ו וַיֹּאמֶר הַמֶּלֶךְ לְאֶסְתֵּר בְּמִשְׁתֵּה הַיַּיִן מַה־שְּׁאֵלָתֵךְ וְיִנָּתֵן לָךְ וּמַה־בַּקָּשָׁתֵךְ עַד־חֲצִי הַמַּלְכוּת וְתֵעָשׂ: ז וַתַּעַן אֶסְתֵּר וַתֹּאמַר שְׁאֵלָתִי וּבַקָּשָׁתִי: ח אִם־מָצָאתִי חֵן בְּעֵינֵי הַמֶּלֶךְ וְאִם־עַל־הַמֶּלֶךְ טוֹב לָתֵת אֶת־שְׁאֵלָתִי וְלַעֲשׂוֹת אֶת־בַּקָּשָׁתִי יָבוֹא הַמֶּלֶךְ וְהָמָן אֶל־הַמִּשְׁתֶּה אֲשֶׁר אֶעֱשֶׂה לָהֶם וּמָחָר אֶעֱשֶׂה כִּדְבַר הַמֶּלֶךְ:

5 The king said, "Get Haman quickly to do what Esther said." And the king and Haman came to the banquet that Esther made. 6 At the banquet, the king said to Esther, "What's your wish? It will be given to you! And what's your request? You can ask for up to half the kingdom and it will be done!" 7 Esther responded and said, "My wish and my request... 8 If I have found compassion in the eyes of the king, and if it pleases Your Majesty to give me what I wish and to do what I request, let the king and Haman come to another banquet that I'll make for them. And tomorrow I'll tell you."

Pasuk 8
Why did Esther invite Ahashverosh and Haman to a second party? Why didn't she just make her request then and there on the first day?

The Vilna Gaon suggests Esther was tricking Haman:

Vilna Gaon (Lithuania, 250 years ago)   אדרת אליהו

She said this so that Haman would think that he was as important to her as he was to the king.

אָמְרָה כֵּן כְּדֵי שֶׁיִּסְבֹּר הָמָן שֶׁהוּא חָשׁוּב מְאֹד בְּעֵינֶיהָ כְּמוֹ בְּעֵינֵי הַמֶּלֶךְ.

• Why would Esther want to make Haman feel important? How would this help her get rid of him and his plot to kill the Jews?

Ibn Ezra thinks that other events affected Esther's decision about when to speak:

Ibn Ezra (Spain, 900 years ago)   אבן עזרא

Esther didn't speak on the first day at the banquet because she had not seen a sign from God in response to the Jews' fast. But when God did great things for Mordekhai on the second day, her heart strengthened.

אִחֲרָה אֶסְתֵּר לְדַבֵּר בַּיּוֹם הָרִאשׁוֹן בְּמִשְׁתֵּה הַיַּיִן, בַּעֲבוּר שֶׁלֹּא רָאֲתָה שׁוּם אוֹת שֶׁחִדֵּשׁ ה' בַּעֲבוּר תַּעֲנִית יִשְׂרָאֵל. וְכַאֲשֶׁר עָשָׂה בַּיּוֹם הַשֵּׁנִי דְּבַר גְּדֻלַּת מָרְדְּכַי חָזֵק לִבָּהּ.

• How many times does it seem Esther is about to ask Ahashverosh for something but then doesn't? How many times does Esther wonder whether the king will listen to her?

• Why might it have been very hard for Esther to talk to the king? Have you ever had trouble saying what's on your mind? Does it sometimes take you more than one try?

• What is Esther looking for? How would Esther get strength from the story of great things happening to Mordekhai? (See pages 62 to 69.)

• Do you ever feel like you experience a "sign" from God that the time is right to do something hard?

ט וַיֵּצֵא הָמָן בַּיּוֹם הַהוּא שָׂמֵחַ וְטוֹב לֵב וְכִרְאוֹת הָמָן אֶת־מָרְדֳּכַי בְּשַׁעַר הַמֶּלֶךְ וְלֹא־קָם
וְלֹא־זָע מִמֶּנּוּ וַיִּמָּלֵא הָמָן עַל־מָרְדֳּכַי חֵמָה: י וַיִּתְאַפַּק הָמָן וַיָּבוֹא אֶל־בֵּיתוֹ וַיִּשְׁלַח וַיָּבֵא
אֶת־אֹהֲבָיו וְאֶת־זֶרֶשׁ אִשְׁתּוֹ: יא וַיְסַפֵּר לָהֶם הָמָן אֶת־כְּבוֹד עָשְׁרוֹ וְרֹב בָּנָיו וְאֵת כָּל־אֲשֶׁר
גִּדְּלוֹ הַמֶּלֶךְ וְאֵת אֲשֶׁר נִשְּׂאוֹ עַל־הַשָּׂרִים וְעַבְדֵי הַמֶּלֶךְ: יב וַיֹּאמֶר הָמָן אַף לֹא־הֵבִיאָה אֶסְתֵּר
הַמַּלְכָּה עִם־הַמֶּלֶךְ אֶל־הַמִּשְׁתֶּה אֲשֶׁר־עָשָׂתָה כִּי אִם־אוֹתִי וְגַם־לְמָחָר אֲנִי קָרוּא־לָהּ עִם־
הַמֶּלֶךְ: יג וְכָל־זֶה אֵינֶנּוּ שֹׁוֶה לִי בְּכָל־עֵת אֲשֶׁר אֲנִי רֹאֶה אֶת־מָרְדֳּכַי הַיְּהוּדִי יוֹשֵׁב בְּשַׁעַר
הַמֶּלֶךְ: יד וַתֹּאמֶר לוֹ זֶרֶשׁ אִשְׁתּוֹ וְכָל־אֹהֲבָיו יַעֲשׂוּ־עֵץ גָּבֹהַּ חֲמִשִּׁים אַמָּה וּבַבֹּקֶר אֱמֹר
לַמֶּלֶךְ וְיִתְלוּ אֶת־מָרְדֳּכַי עָלָיו וּבֹא עִם־הַמֶּלֶךְ אֶל־הַמִּשְׁתֶּה שָׂמֵחַ וַיִּיטַב הַדָּבָר לִפְנֵי הָמָן
וַיַּעַשׂ הָעֵץ:

9 Haman left that day happy and feeling great. But when Haman saw Mordekhai in the king's court—not getting up or moving for him—Haman was filled with anger toward Mordekhai. 10 But Haman held himself back and went home. He brought over his friends and Zeresh, his wife. 11 Haman told them about the honor of his wealth and about how great his sons were and about how the king promoted him and raised him up over the other advisors and servants. 12 Haman said, "I'm the only person that Queen Esther invited to attend the banquet—that she made—with the king. And I'm also invited tomorrow—with the king! 13 But none of this is worth anything to me as long as I see Mordekhai the Jew sitting in the king's court." 14 Haman's wife, Zeresh, and all his friends said to him, "Let them make a wooden post 50 amot (about 75 feet!) high. In the morning, talk to the king and they will hang Mordekhai on it. Then you can be happy when you go to the banquet with the king." Haman thought this was a great idea, and he made the post.

Pasuk 11
Haman lists so many incredible things he has in life. He's rich, he has honor, he's powerful, he has a great family. He has it all! How can Haman say that none of that is worth anything to him just because of Mordekhai not bowing to him?

Ralbag suggests two possibilities:

1 Ralbag (France, 700 years ago)

He means to say that all this honor and greatness is worthless to him because of his tremendous anger about Mordekhai not giving him honor.

רלב"ג

רוֹצֶה לוֹמַר שֶׁכָּל זֶה הַכָּבוֹד וְזֹאת הַגְּדֻלָּה לֹא יִשְׁווּ לִי לַכַּעַס אֲשֶׁר אֲנִי כּוֹעֵס עַל מָרְדְּכַי הַיְהוּדִי בִּרְאוֹתִי שֶׁאֵינוֹ נִכְנָע לָתֶת לִי כָּבוֹד.

Being angry can really mess up your perspective on what's important. Ralbag suggests that Haman's anger prevents him from seeing how special all his blessings are. This is sometimes called being "blinded by rage."

- Do you ever feel that way? Have you ever been really upset or angry over something that was ultimately not that big of a deal?

- Did you ever lose sight of what was really important because you were angry?

- What does this teach us about Haman? What advice would you give him?

2 Or perhaps he meant that even though he does appreciate all his blessings, he just can't enjoy them because of how much it bothers him when Mordekhai doesn't show him honor.

אוֹ יִרְצֶה בָּזֶה שֶׁכָּל הַכָּבוֹד אֵינוֹ מוֹעִיל לִי מֵרֹב הַהִפָּעֲלוּת אֲשֶׁר לִי עַל מָרְדְּכַי בִּרְאוֹתִי אוֹתוֹ שֶׁאֵינוֹ נִכְנָע לָתֶת לִי כָּבוֹד.

Sometimes you'd like to enjoy an experience or a moment, but something is really bothering you, and you just can't get it out of your mind. Ralbag suggests this went way too far with Haman. He knew better, but he couldn't let himself enjoy his blessings because he was obsessing too much about Mordekhai.

- Have you ever felt so distracted by something that wasn't so important? Did that ever prevent you from being able to appreciate other good things around you?

- What do we miss out on when we let small things take over our thoughts? How can we refocus on what's really important and be more "in the moment"?

- Can both of Ralbag's suggestions be true at the same time? How so?

CHAPTER 6   פֶּרֶק ו

הַהוּא נָדְדָה שְׁנַת הַמֶּלֶךְ וַיֹּאמֶר לְהָבִיא אֶת־סֵפֶר הַזִּכְרֹנוֹת דִּבְרֵי הַיָּמִים וַיִּהְיוּ נִקְרָאִים לִפְנֵי הַמֶּלֶךְ:

1 That night, the king's sleep was disturbed. He asked for the book of history to be read before him.

DID YOU KNOW? When reading this pasuk, some Megillah readers have the custom of singing the word הַמֶּלֶךְ (ha-melekh, the king) to the tune used to sing that word in the beginning of Shaharit on Rosh Hashanah and Yom Kippur. In the tefillah there, the word is definitely talking about God!

שְׁאֵלוֹת
Scavenger Hunt

FIND THE ANSWERS IN CHAPTER 6!

1. After Ahashverosh finds out that Mordekhai was not rewarded for saving his life, what is his next question?

2. What did Haman call out as he paraded Mordekhai around town?

3. Who was in mourning?

4. What did Zeresh and Haman's friends say to him?

Pasuk 1
Whose sleep was disturbed?

The Gemara records a מַחֲלֹקֶת (mahloket, debate) about how to understand this.

Talmud Bavli Megillah 15b	**תלמוד בבלי מגילה דף טו עמוד ב**
R. Tanhum said: The sleep of the King of the world was disturbed….	אָמַר רַבִּי תַּנְחוּם: נָדְדָה שְׁנַת מַלְכּוֹ שֶׁל עוֹלָם….
Rava said: It was the sleep of the actual King Ahashverosh.	רָבָא אָמַר: שְׁנַת הַמֶּלֶךְ אֲחַשְׁוֵרוֹשׁ מַמָּשׁ.

- Why do you think Ahashverosh might have had a tough time sleeping that night? What might have been on his mind? Could it be something Esther said or did in perek 5, or something else?

- What would it mean for God's sleep to be disturbed? Why could the story up until this point be described as a time of "God sleeping," and why could the story after this point be described as a time of "God being awake"?

This mahloket connects to a midrash:

Esther Rabbah 3:10	**אסתר רבה ג:י**
R. Yudan and R. Levi said in the name of R. Yohanan: Wherever it says in this Megillah "of King Ahashverosh" (like in 1:9), it's talking about King Ahashverosh. But wherever it just says "of the king," we don't know. It might be referring to Ahashverosh, or it might be referring to God!	רַבִּי יוּדָן וְרַבִּי לֵוִי בְּשֵׁם רַבִּי יוֹחָנָן, כָּל מָקוֹם שֶׁנֶּאֱמַר בִּמְגִלָּה זוֹ לַמֶּלֶךְ אֲחַשְׁוֵרוֹשׁ, בַּמֶּלֶךְ אֲחַשְׁוֵרוֹשׁ הַכָּתוּב מְדַבֵּר, וְכָל מָקוֹם שֶׁנֶּאֱמַר לַמֶּלֶךְ סְתָם, מְשַׁמֵּשׁ קֹדֶשׁ וָחֹל.

- How would it change the Megillah to read some references to "the king" as talking about God?

- TRY IT OUT! Find the word מֶלֶךְ (melekh, king) as you read through the Megillah. Can you find times where it's possible to interpret this word as talking about God?

- Other than these kinds of clues, God doesn't seem to be in the Megillah! Do you want to know why not? Look at page 55.

כ וַיִּמָּצֵא כָתוּב אֲשֶׁר הִגִּיד מָרְדֳּכַי עַל־בִּגְתָנָא וָתֶרֶשׁ שְׁנֵי סָרִיסֵי הַמֶּלֶךְ מִשֹּׁמְרֵי הַסַּף אֲשֶׁר בִּקְשׁוּ לִשְׁלֹחַ יָד בַּמֶּלֶךְ אֲחַשְׁוֵרוֹשׁ: ג וַיֹּאמֶר הַמֶּלֶךְ מַה־נַּעֲשָׂה יְקָר וּגְדוּלָּה לְמָרְדֳּכַי עַל־זֶה וַיֹּאמְרוּ נַעֲרֵי הַמֶּלֶךְ מְשָׁרְתָיו לֹא־נַעֲשָׂה עִמּוֹ דָּבָר:

2 They came to the part where it was written that Mordekhai uncovered Bigtan and Teresh's plot to murder the king. 3 The king asked, "What amazing honor was done for Mordekhai for this?" The servants replied, "Nothing was done for him!"

- Do you think it might have been hard for Esther to give credit to Mordekhai? Why might she have wanted to take credit for saving the king's life herself? What can this story tell us about Esther's character and personality?

- Besides for the chance that you might save your whole people, why else is it important to give credit for words you heard from someone? If Hazal felt the redemption of the world is at stake, what does that tell you about the importance of being honest and giving credit where credit is due?

Don't thank me, thank Mordekhai.

Pasuk 2
How did the story of Mordekhai saving Ahashverosh end up in the king's book of history?

It's because, back in perek 2, even though it was Esther who told Ahashverosh about Bigtan and Teresh's plot, she made sure to give credit to Mordekhai for discovering it. Our Rabbis learn an important value from Esther:

Talmud Bavli Megillah 15a

R. Elazar said in the name of R. Hanina: Anyone who says something giving credit to the one who first said it brings redemption to the world, as it says, "Esther told the king, giving credit to Mordekhai" (Esther 2:22).

תלמוד בבלי מגילה דף טו עמוד א

וְאָמַר רַבִּי אֶלְעָזָר אָמַר רַבִּי חֲנִינָא: כָּל הָאוֹמֵר דָּבָר בְּשֵׁם אוֹמְרוֹ מֵבִיא גְאוּלָה לָעוֹלָם, שֶׁנֶּאֱמַר: "וַתֹּאמֶר אֶסְתֵּר לַמֶּלֶךְ בְּשֵׁם מָרְדֳּכָי."

It's important to give credit, like when you're repeating someone else's words. In the Megillah, Esther giving proper credit to Mordekhai helped save the Jews!

ד וַיֹּאמֶר הַמֶּלֶךְ מִי בֶחָצֵר וְהָמָן בָּא לַחֲצַר בֵּית־הַמֶּלֶךְ הַחִיצוֹנָה לֵאמֹר
לַמֶּלֶךְ לִתְלוֹת אֶת־מָרְדֳּכַי עַל־הָעֵץ אֲשֶׁר־הֵכִין לוֹ: ה וַיֹּאמְרוּ נַעֲרֵי הַמֶּלֶךְ
אֵלָיו הִנֵּה הָמָן עֹמֵד בֶּחָצֵר וַיֹּאמֶר הַמֶּלֶךְ יָבוֹא: ו וַיָּבוֹא הָמָן וַיֹּאמֶר לוֹ
הַמֶּלֶךְ מַה־לַעֲשׂוֹת בָּאִישׁ אֲשֶׁר הַמֶּלֶךְ חָפֵץ בִּיקָרוֹ וַיֹּאמֶר הָמָן בְּלִבּוֹ
לְמִי יַחְפֹּץ הַמֶּלֶךְ לַעֲשׂוֹת יְקָר יוֹתֵר מִמֶּנִּי: ז וַיֹּאמֶר הָמָן אֶל־הַמֶּלֶךְ אִישׁ
אֲשֶׁר הַמֶּלֶךְ חָפֵץ בִּיקָרוֹ: ח יָבִיאוּ לְבוּשׁ מַלְכוּת אֲשֶׁר לָבַשׁ־בּוֹ הַמֶּלֶךְ
וְסוּס אֲשֶׁר רָכַב עָלָיו הַמֶּלֶךְ וַאֲשֶׁר נִתַּן כֶּתֶר מַלְכוּת בְּרֹאשׁוֹ: ט וְנָתוֹן
הַלְּבוּשׁ וְהַסּוּס עַל־יַד־אִישׁ מִשָּׂרֵי הַמֶּלֶךְ הַפַּרְתְּמִים וְהִלְבִּישׁוּ אֶת־הָאִישׁ
אֲשֶׁר הַמֶּלֶךְ חָפֵץ בִּיקָרוֹ וְהִרְכִּיבֻהוּ עַל־הַסּוּס בִּרְחוֹב הָעִיר וְקָרְאוּ לְפָנָיו
כָּכָה יֵעָשֶׂה לָאִישׁ אֲשֶׁר הַמֶּלֶךְ חָפֵץ בִּיקָרוֹ:

4 The king said, "Who's in the courtyard?" It was Haman, coming to ask the king to hang Mordekhai on the post he had prepared. 5 The king's servants said to him, "Oh look, Haman is standing in the courtyard." The king said, "He should come in." 6 Haman came, and the king said to him, "What should be done for someone whom the king wants to honor?" Haman thought to himself, "The king must be talking about me! Who else could it be?" 7 Haman said to the king, "For a person whom the king wants to honor, 8 get the king's royal robes, the king's horse, and his crown. 9 Give the clothing and the horse to one of the high-ranking ministers, and they should dress the person the king wants to honor and parade him on a horse through the town square and call out before him, 'This is what is done to a person whom the king wants to honor!'"

י וַיֹּאמֶר הַמֶּלֶךְ לְהָמָן מַהֵר קַח אֶת־הַלְּבוּשׁ וְאֶת־הַסּוּס כַּאֲשֶׁר דִּבַּרְתָּ וַעֲשֵׂה־כֵן לְמָרְדֳּכַי הַיְּהוּדִי הַיּוֹשֵׁב בְּשַׁעַר הַמֶּלֶךְ אַל־תַּפֵּל דָּבָר מִכֹּל אֲשֶׁר דִּבַּרְתָּ:

10 The king said to Haman, "Quick! Grab the clothing and the horse as you said, and do all that for Mordekhai the Jew who sits in the king's court. Don't leave out one thing you said!"

- Why is it such an honor for someone to wear the king's clothing and ride the king's horse? How is that related to the horse having a crown and the law that no one else was ever allowed to ride that horse?

- Isn't it a little unusual to wear someone else's clothing? What does this tell us about the relationship between people and their clothing? Can you find other places in the Megillah where clothing are a big part of the story? What do you think we can learn from that?

- There is a tradition of dressing up in costumes on Purim (Shu"t Mahar"i Mintz, 15). How might that connect to the Purim story?

Pasuk 10
Ahashverosh tells Haman to grab the fancy clothing and horse, just as Haman had suggested. But in pasuk 8 Haman actually said to get three things: "the king's royal robes, the king's horse, and his crown." What happened to the crown?

It's possible the crown is included in הַלְּבוּשׁ (the clothing). Here are two other answers:

1 | **Ibn Ezra (Spain, 900 years ago)**

Some say the king was angry that Haman included the crown, because it was an insult to his royal honor. That's why Haman said (in pasuk 9), "Give the clothing and the horse," and he didn't mention the crown again.

אבן עזרא אסתר ו:ח

יֵשׁ אוֹמְרִים שֶׁהִרְגִּישׁ שֶׁחָרָה עַל הַמֶּלֶךְ עַל כֶּתֶר הַמַּלְכוּת בַּעֲבוּר כְּבוֹד הַמַּלְכוּת, עַל כֵּן אָמַר "וְנָתוֹן הַלְּבוּשׁ וְהַסּוּס" וְלֹא הִזְכִּיר הַכֶּתֶר.

In Ibn Ezra's first answer, Haman went too far when he suggested that someone else could wear the royal crown.

- Why would Ahashverosh be angry with Haman for making that suggestion?

- Remember, Haman thought that he was going to get all this. What does it say about him that he wanted to wear the king's crown? Could this change how much Ahashverosh trusts Haman?

2 But I think the correct answer is that in Haman's original suggestion, "his crown" refers to the horse! Sometimes a horse belonging to a king has a crown that it wears while the king rides on it. This makes it forbidden for anyone else to ride that horse.

וְהַנָּכוֹן בְּעֵינַי שֶׁוְּ"ו בְּרֹאשׁוֹ שָׁב אֶל הַסּוּס כִּי יֵשׁ סוּס שֶׁל הַמֶּלֶךְ שֶׁיָּשִׂימוּ כֶּתֶר מַלְכוּת בְּרֹאשׁוֹ, וְאֵין אֶחָד מֵעַבְדֵי הַמֶּלֶךְ רַשַּׁאי לִרְכֹּב עָלָיו.

According to Ibn Ezra's second answer, the crown wasn't mentioned in our pasuk because it was included with the horse. And the crown on the horse shows that riding that horse (and wearing the king's clothing) was a really big deal!

יא וַיִּקַּח הָמָן אֶת־הַלְּבוּשׁ וְאֶת־הַסּוּס וַיַּלְבֵּשׁ אֶת־מָרְדֳּכַי וַיַּרְכִּיבֵהוּ בִּרְחוֹב הָעִיר וַיִּקְרָא לְפָנָיו כָּכָה יֵעָשֶׂה לָאִישׁ אֲשֶׁר הַמֶּלֶךְ חָפֵץ בִּיקָרוֹ:

11 Haman took the clothing and the horse and dressed Mordekhai. Haman paraded him through the town square, calling out before him, "This is what is done to a person whom the king wants to honor!"

Pasuk 11

Compare Mordekhai's ride on the horse to this description of Yosef, when he became second-in-command to Pharaoh in מִצְרַיִם (Mitzrayim, Egypt):

Bereishit 41:42–43

Pharaoh took the ring off his finger and handed it to Yosef. He had him dressed in robes of fine linen and put a gold chain around his neck.

He had him ride in the chariot of the second-in-command, and an "avreikh" announced him.

He was placed in charge of all of Mitzrayim.

בראשית מא:מב–מג

וַיָּסַר פַּרְעֹה אֶת טַבַּעְתּוֹ מֵעַל יָדוֹ וַיִּתֵּן אֹתָהּ עַל יַד יוֹסֵף וַיַּלְבֵּשׁ אֹתוֹ בִּגְדֵי שֵׁשׁ וַיָּשֶׂם רְבִד הַזָּהָב עַל צַוָּארוֹ:

וַיַּרְכֵּב אֹתוֹ בְּמִרְכֶּבֶת הַמִּשְׁנֶה אֲשֶׁר לוֹ וַיִּקְרְאוּ לְפָנָיו אַבְרֵךְ וְנָתוֹן אֹתוֹ עַל כָּל אֶרֶץ מִצְרָיִם:

It's unclear exactly what "avreikh" means, but the ancient Jewish historian Josephus says it's a "herald," which is an official announcer or messenger.

- Which details in these pesukim about Yosef also appear in the Purim story?

- How do you think Mordekhai felt when he was being dressed up and paraded around? Was it enjoyable for him? How might his feelings have been similar to Yosef's, and in what ways were their experiences different?

- The Yosef story and the Purim story are both about Jewish leaders who rise to power under non-Jewish kings and end up saving their people. There are other details these stories share, such as secrets and hidden identities, good deeds being forgotten, and an emphasis on beauty. Can you find these details or others in both stories?

יב וַיָּשָׁב מָרְדֳּכַי אֶל־שַׁעַר הַמֶּלֶךְ וְהָמָן נִדְחַף אֶל־בֵּיתוֹ אָבֵל וַחֲפוּי רֹאשׁ: יג וַיְסַפֵּר הָמָן לְזֶרֶשׁ אִשְׁתּוֹ וּלְכָל־אֹהֲבָיו אֵת כָּל־אֲשֶׁר קָרָהוּ וַיֹּאמְרוּ לוֹ חֲכָמָיו וְזֶרֶשׁ אִשְׁתּוֹ אִם מִזֶּרַע הַיְּהוּדִים מָרְדֳּכַי אֲשֶׁר הַחִלּוֹתָ לִנְפֹּל לְפָנָיו לֹא־תוּכַל לוֹ כִּי־נָפוֹל תִּפּוֹל לְפָנָיו: יד עוֹדָם מְדַבְּרִים עִמּוֹ וְסָרִיסֵי הַמֶּלֶךְ הִגִּיעוּ וַיַּבְהִלוּ לְהָבִיא אֶת־הָמָן אֶל־הַמִּשְׁתֶּה אֲשֶׁר־עָשְׂתָה אֶסְתֵּר:

12 After that, Mordekhai went back to the king's court. Haman rushed home, mournful and face fallen. 13 Haman told all his friends and his wife, Zeresh, about everything that happened. They said to him, "If Mordekhai is Jewish, and you've started falling before him, then you won't be able to beat him. You'll surely keep falling." 14 They were in the middle of talking to him, and suddenly the king's servants arrived in a commotion to take Haman to Esther's banquet.

Pasuk 12
What happened after Mordekhai's ride on the king's horse?

Esther Rabbah 10:6–7	**אסתר רבה י:ו–ז**
"Mordekhai went back to the king's court"—this teaches that he returned to his rags and to his fasting....	"וַיָּשָׁב מָרְדֳּכַי אֶל שַׁעַר הַמֶּלֶךְ" — מְלַמֵּד שֶׁשָּׁב לְשַׂקּוֹ וּלְתַעֲנִיתוֹ....
"Haman rushed home, mournful and face fallen"—mourning about his house, face fallen about what happened.	"וְהָמָן נִדְחַף אֶל בֵּיתוֹ אָבֵל וַחֲפוּי רֹאשׁ"—אָבֵל עַל בֵּיתוֹ, וַחֲפוּי רֹאשׁ עַל מַה שֶּׁקָּרָהוּ.

- Mordekhai has just been honored by the king and driven around town by Haman. Why is he not happier about this? Why does he return to what he was doing before, as if nothing has changed?

- What does this teach us about how important this honor was to Mordekhai? How does this contrast to Haman's attitude toward being honored in 6:6?

  - Haman is beginning to realize that things are not going his way. What is he worried about, and why?

  - In pasuk 13, Haman's friends and his wife, Zeresh, begin to doubt that Haman will get out of this alive. How might it feel for Haman to hear his wife and friends talk to him this way?

CHAPTER 7 פֶּרֶק ז

הַמֶּלֶךְ וְהָמָן לִשְׁתּוֹת עִם־אֶסְתֵּר הַמַּלְכָּה: ב וַיֹּאמֶר הַמֶּלֶךְ לְאֶסְתֵּר גַּם בַּיּוֹם הַשֵּׁנִי בְּמִשְׁתֵּה הַיַּיִן מַה־שְּׁאֵלָתֵךְ אֶסְתֵּר הַמַּלְכָּה וְתִנָּתֵן לָךְ וּמַה־בַּקָּשָׁתֵךְ עַד־חֲצִי הַמַּלְכוּת וְתֵעָשׂ:

1 So the king and Haman came to feast with Queen Esther. 2 The king said to Esther again on that second day, "What's your wish, Queen Esther? It will be given to you! And what's your request? You can ask for up to half the kingdom and it will be done."

שְׁאֵלוֹת
?
Scavenger Hunt

FIND THE ANSWERS IN CHAPTER 7!

1. If the Jewish people were only being sold into slavery rather than being killed, what does Esther say she would do?

2. Why did the king go to the palace garden?

3. There is an unusual, rare note in this chapter. On what word does it appear?

4. Who told Ahashverosh that Haman had a post ready for hanging Mordekhai?

ג וַתַּעַן אֶסְתֵּר הַמַּלְכָּה וַתֹּאמַר אִם־מָצָאתִי חֵן בְּעֵינֶיךָ הַמֶּלֶךְ וְאִם־עַל־הַמֶּלֶךְ טוֹב תִּנָּתֶן־לִי נַפְשִׁי בִּשְׁאֵלָתִי וְעַמִּי בְּבַקָּשָׁתִי: ד כִּי נִמְכַּרְנוּ אֲנִי וְעַמִּי לְהַשְׁמִיד לַהֲרוֹג וּלְאַבֵּד וְאִלּוּ לַעֲבָדִים וְלִשְׁפָחוֹת נִמְכַּרְנוּ הֶחֱרַשְׁתִּי כִּי אֵין הַצָּר שֹׁוֶה בְּנֵזֶק הַמֶּלֶךְ: ה וַיֹּאמֶר הַמֶּלֶךְ אֲחַשְׁוֵרוֹשׁ וַיֹּאמֶר לְאֶסְתֵּר הַמַּלְכָּה מִי הוּא זֶה וְאֵי־זֶה הוּא אֲשֶׁר־מְלָאוֹ לִבּוֹ לַעֲשׂוֹת כֵּן:

3 Queen Esther answered, "If I have found compassion in Your Majesty's eyes, and if it pleases Your Majesty: My wish is for my life, and my request is for my people. 4 For we have been sold out to be destroyed, murdered, and annihilated. If we had only been sold as slaves, I wouldn't have said anything. But killing us does not benefit the king." 5 King Ahashverosh said to Queen Esther, "Who on earth would dare to do such a thing?!"

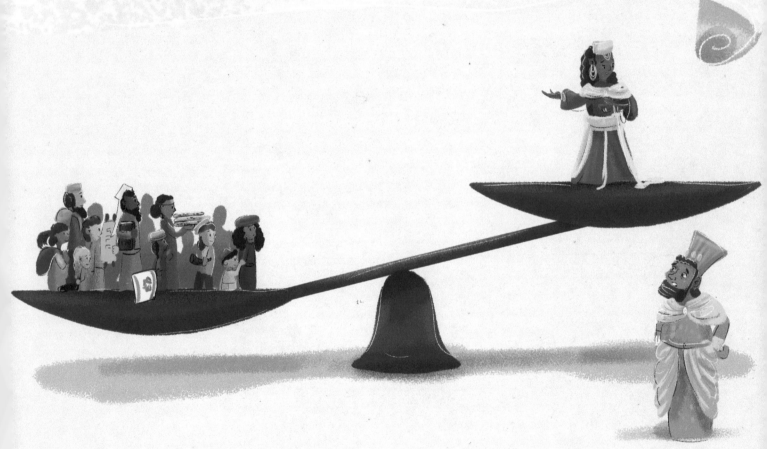

- Have you ever been on an airplane? Before takeoff, they make an announcement that if people need to wear oxygen masks to help breathe better, adults should put their own masks on first before helping other people like their kids. What are other examples of when you'd need to help yourself before others, and when is it better to help others before yourself?

- Some people are really good at doing things themselves. As we grow up and become more capable, we like to be the ones to help! But it's important to remember: Sometimes we need help too, and that's okay. How does Esther teach this to us?

Pasuk 3
Why does Esther ask Ahashverosh first to save herself and only then to save her people?

Here are two possibilities from our פַּרְשָׁנִים (parshanim, commentators):

Malbim (Eastern Europe, 200 years ago)

מלבי"ם

The שְׁאֵלָה (she'eilah, wish) is what it's called when Esther asks for her own life, but a בַּקָשָׁה (bakashah, request) is what it's called when she asks for others…. Saving her people was more important to Esther than her own life, and she would have agreed for herself to be killed as long as they would be saved. That's why her she'eilah is for herself and why she later says, "How can I bear to see the evil that will happen to my people" (8:6). The main goal of the request was not about her, but about her people.

הַשְּׁאֵלָה הִיא מַה שֶּׁתְּבַקֵּשׁ לְצֹרֶךְ עַצְמָהּ, וְהַבַּקָשָׁה הִיא מָה שֶּׁתְּבַקֵּשׁ לְצֹרֶךְ אֲחֵרִים…. כָּל כָּךְ יָקָר בְּעֵינֶיהָ הַצָּלַת עַמָּהּ עַד שֶׁהָיְתָה מַסְכֶּמֶת שֶׁתֹּאבַד הִיא בִּלְבַד שֶׁעַמָּהּ יִנָּצְלוּ, בְּאֹפֶן שֶׁהַשְּׁאֵלָה אֶל הַמֶּלֶךְ תִּהְיֶה בַּעֲבוּר עַצְמָהּ כְּמוֹ שֶׁכָּתוּב "כִּי אֵיכָכָה אוּכַל וְרָאִיתִי" — אֲבָל עִקַּר הַבַּקָשָׁה וְתַכְלִיתָהּ הוּא עַמָּהּ.

Malbim says our pasuk shows that Esther asks for her own life separately from the rest of the people because they are **not** equally important to her. Asking for her own life was just a שְׁאֵלָה (she'eilah, wish), but asking for others was a בַּקָשָׁה (bakashah, request), which was her most important goal. Later, when she repeats this request in perek 8, she's really saying: I can't bear to see them killed, and if you will only save one or the other, save them.

- It's not common to have heroes like Esther, people who are willing to give up everything in order to save other people. Can you think of some examples?

- Why would Esther be willing to trade her life for ours? What does that teach us about Esther?

R. Moshe Alshikh (Eretz Yisrael, 500 years ago)

משאת משה

She knew in her heart that a prisoner cannot free themselves and others at the same time. Therefore she said: Grant me my life first as my wish and then, afterward, once I am safely off the boat, grant my people's lives for my request.

אָמְרָה בְּלִבָּהּ הֲלֹא אֵין חָבוּשׁ מַתִּיר עַצְמוֹ וּמָה גַּם אֶת אֲחֵרִים, עַל כֵּן אָמְרָה תִּנָּתֶן לִי נַפְשִׁי תְּחִלָּה בִּשְׁאֵלָתִי וְאַחַר כָּךְ שֶׁאֶהְיֶה חוּץ לַסִּירָה וְעַמִּי בְּבַקָּשָׁתִי.

R. Alshikh teaches that Esther's request is connected to an idea we learn from the Talmud Bavli: A prisoner cannot free themselves from prison (Berakhot 5b). Esther needed to save herself before she would be able to save all of her people. Sometimes, if we want to be in a position to help other people, we have to make sure we are safe and able to do that first.

ו וַתֹּאמֶר אֶסְתֵּר אִישׁ צַר וְאוֹיֵב הָמָן הָרָע הַזֶּה וְהָמָן נִבְעַת מִלִּפְנֵי הַמֶּלֶךְ וְהַמַּלְכָּה: ז וְהַמֶּלֶךְ קָם בַּחֲמָתוֹ מִמִּשְׁתֵּה הַיַּיִן אֶל־גִּנַּת הַבִּיתָן וְהָמָן עָמַד לְבַקֵּשׁ עַל־נַפְשׁוֹ מֵאֶסְתֵּר הַמַּלְכָּה כִּי רָאָה כִּי־כָלְתָה אֵלָיו הָרָעָה מֵאֵת הַמֶּלֶךְ: ח וְהַמֶּלֶךְ שָׁב מִגִּנַּת הַבִּיתָן אֶל־בֵּית מִשְׁתֵּה הַיַּיִן וְהָמָן נֹפֵל עַל־הַמִּטָּה אֲשֶׁר אֶסְתֵּר עָלֶיהָ וַיֹּאמֶר הַמֶּלֶךְ הֲגַם לִכְבּוֹשׁ אֶת־הַמַּלְכָּה עִמִּי בַּבָּיִת הַדָּבָר יָצָא מִפִּי הַמֶּלֶךְ וּפְנֵי הָמָן חָפוּ:

6 Esther said, "A tyrant and an enemy–this wicked Haman right here!!" And Haman was trembling before the king and queen. 7 The king rose up in fury from the banquet and went out to the palace garden. Haman saw that the king had it in for him now, so he stood to beg Queen Esther for his life. 8 The king came back from the garden and just then Haman fell into Esther's couch. The king said, "Are you even trying to conquer the queen right in front of me?!" As soon as he said it, Haman's face fell in horror.

Commentary

Pasuk 7
Why did Ahashverosh go out to his garden in the middle of a really tense moment?

R. Yosef ibn Yahya (Italy, 500 years ago)

In order to get some relief in the garden and to cool off a little from the heat of his anger.

ר׳ יוֹסֵף אבן יחייא

כְּדֵי לָקַחַת קוֹרַת רוּחַ בַּגִּנָּה וּלְהִתְקָרֵר מְעַט מֵחֲמַת וְחוֹם כַּעֲסוֹ.

If you get angry, it's usually a good idea to take some time to yourself and think it through before you make decisions or take actions you'll regret later.

- Why does Ahashverosh seem torn, though? What was he struggling with? If you found out that your closest advisor was trying to kill your spouse and their whole people, would it be hard to know what to do?

- What does this say about how much Ahashverosh really cared about Esther?

- What would have happened if Ahashverosh did let his anger calm down?

In this case, that didn't happen! According to the Gemara, God sent angels to make sure that Ahashverosh came back just as angry as when he left:

Talmud Bavli Megillah 16a

He went outside and found angels there that looked to him like people, and they were uprooting the trees of the garden.

He said to them, "What are you doing?!"

They said to him, "What Haman commanded us!"

תלמוד בבלי מגילה דף טז עמוד א

דַּאֲזַל וְאַשְׁכַּח לְמַלְאֲכֵי הַשָּׁרֵת דְּאִידְּמוּ לֵיהּ כְּגַבְרֵי, וְקָא עָקְרִי לְאִילָנֵי דְּבוּסְתָּנֵי,

וַאֲמַר לְהוּ: מַאי עוֹבָדַיְיכוּ?

אֲמַרוּ לֵיהּ: דְּפַקְּדִינַן הָמָן.

- This midrash suggests that God was doing something behind the scenes to protect the Jewish people. Can you think of other times in the Megillah when God might have been arranging small miracles to make sure the Jewish people were saved in the end? (See page 55 for more about God's role in the Purim story.)

ט וַיֹּאמֶר חַרְבוֹנָה אֶחָד מִן־הַסָּרִיסִים לִפְנֵי הַמֶּלֶךְ גַּם הִנֵּה־הָעֵץ אֲשֶׁר־עָשָׂה הָמָן לְמׇרְדֳּכַי אֲשֶׁר דִּבֶּר־טוֹב עַל־הַמֶּלֶךְ עֹמֵד בְּבֵית הָמָן גָּבֹהַּ חֲמִשִּׁים אַמָּה וַיֹּאמֶר הַמֶּלֶךְ תְּלֻהוּ עָלָיו: י וַיִּתְלוּ אֶת־הָמָן עַל־הָעֵץ אֲשֶׁר־הֵכִין לְמׇרְדֳּכָי וַחֲמַת הַמֶּלֶךְ שָׁכָכָה:

9 Harvonah, one of the king's servants, spoke up and said, "There's this 50-amot-high post that Haman made to hang Mordekhai, who's the one who spoke well of the king." And the king said, "Hang Haman on it!" 10 So they hanged Haman on the post he had planned for Mordekhai. And the king wasn't angry anymore.

1-Minute Debate · דַּקָּה שֶׁל דִּיּוּן

Harvonah was a good guy. ??? ???

Disagree!

o He seems to know a lot about Haman's plan, even down to the exact height of the post he made to hang Mordekhai! That's very suspicious.

o If he was such a good guy, why didn't he say anything until now?

o In 1:10, he's listed as one of the advisors Ahashverosh sends to take Vashti to his party when she doesn't want to go. Doesn't sound like such a good guy to me.

Agree!

o Who says the Harvonah in perek 7 is the same as the one in perek 1? They spell their names completely differently!

o He's the one who pushes Ahashverosh to finally get rid of Haman! If not for him, who knows how Haman might have weaseled out of it?

o Sometimes it's really hard to say the right thing in a stressful moment. Harvonah is a model to us all.

Pasuk 9

Harvonah appears twice in the Megillah. First he's part of a list of Ahashverosh's seven advisors, and his name is spelled with an alef at the end: חַרְבוֹנָא (Esther 1:10). Now he's the one who suggests to Ahashverosh that Haman should be hanged on the post that was intended for Mordekhai. This time his name is spelled with a heh at the end: חַרְבוֹנָה. Was Harvonah a good guy or a bad guy?

Hazal disagree about this:

Yalkut Shimoni on Na"kh

R. Hama bar Hanina said: The evil Harvonah was an accomplice in Haman's plot. But once he saw that it was not going to work out, he immediately switched sides....

Rav said: Harvonah should be remembered for good, and there are those who say that at that very moment Eliyahu ha-Navi (Elijah the prophet) came and appeared as Harvonah. He said to the king: "There is a beam 50 amot (cubits) high from the destroyed Kodesh HaKodashim (the holiest place in the Beit HaMikdash) at Haman's house. May the king command to hang him on it."

ילקוט שמעוני נ״ך תתרנ״ט

אָמַר רַבִּי חָמָא בַּר חֲנִינָא אַף חַרְבוֹנָה הָרָשָׁע בְּאוֹתָהּ עֵצָה הָיָה, כֵּיוָן שֶׁרָאָה שֶׁלֹּא נִתְקַיְּמָה עֲצָתוֹ מִיָּד בָּרַח....

רַב אָמַר חַרְבוֹנָה זָכוּר לַטּוֹב, וְיֵשׁ אוֹמְרִים בְּאוֹתָהּ שָׁעָה בָּא אֵלִיָּהוּ זַ״ל וְנִדְמָה לְחַרְבוֹנָה, אָמַר אֲדֹנִי הַמֶּלֶךְ יֵשׁ עֵץ אֶחָד בְּבֵיתוֹ מִבֵּית קֹדֶשׁ הַקֳּדָשִׁים גָּבוֹהַּ חֲמִשִּׁים אַמָּה יְצַוֶּה הַמֶּלֶךְ לִתְלוֹתוֹ.

R. Hama bar Hanina thinks Harvonah was a coward who had no problem being Haman's accomplice as long as he thought he could get away with it.

Rav thinks Harvonah was a good guy. The Shoshanat Yaakov song that's sung after Megillah reading at shul (page 108) agrees with Rav. It concludes: וְגַם חַרְבוֹנָה זָכוּר לַטּוֹב (and may Harvonah also be remembered for good!).

- According to the second view, what did Harvonah do that was so good? What might have happened if he had said nothing? What can this teach us about speaking up when you have something to say that might help?

- Can you find or think of evidence for both R. Hama and Rav?

- Why do you think this midrash adds the detail about Haman's post coming from the destroyed Beit HaMikdash? How does that change our understanding of the story?

CHAPTER 8   פֶּרֶק ח

בַּיּוֹם הַהוּא נָתַן הַמֶּלֶךְ אֲחַשְׁוֵרוֹשׁ לְאֶסְתֵּר הַמַּלְכָּה אֶת־בֵּית הָמָן צֹרֵר הַיְּהוּדִים וּמָרְדֳּכַי בָּא לִפְנֵי הַמֶּלֶךְ כִּי־הִגִּידָה אֶסְתֵּר מַה הוּא־לָהּ: ב וַיָּסַר הַמֶּלֶךְ אֶת־טַבַּעְתּוֹ אֲשֶׁר הֶעֱבִיר מֵהָמָן וַיִּתְּנָהּ לְמָרְדֳּכָי וַתָּשֶׂם אֶסְתֵּר אֶת־מָרְדֳּכַי עַל־בֵּית הָמָן:

1 On that day, King Ahashverosh gave Queen Esther the household of Haman, enemy of the Jews, and Mordekhai came before the king because Esther told him how they were related. 2 The king took his ring that he had removed from Haman and gave it to Mordekhai. Esther appointed Mordekhai in charge of Haman's household.

פְּשָׁט Reading the Verses

Pesukim 2–3
Haman has been killed, and all his household was given to Esther. It seems like the terrible times are all over. But Esther is still very worried. She cries and begs Ahashverosh to cancel Haman's evil plot. Why is she so nervous about that? Didn't the plot end when Haman died?

According to Ibn Ezra (Spain, 900 years ago), Persian law wouldn't allow a decree to be canceled. So, even though Haman had been killed, the decree to kill the Jews was still there, and Esther needed Ahashverosh to make an exception to the law and cancel the old decree.

Rashi (France, 1,000 years ago) thinks that a decree in Persia could be canceled, but Esther was worried that the king wouldn't want to have his decree overturned because it's disrespectful to reverse something the king already said. So, even though Haman was gone, she still needed Ahashverosh to agree to save the Jews!

- When you read pesukim 3–8, do you see what these פַּרְשָׁנִים (parshanim, commentators) are noticing?

- According to these parshanim, who has more power in the story: Ahashverosh or Haman? Who is more responsible for the threat to the Jewish people?

- How does this change the way you understand Megillat Esther?

שְׁאֵלוֹת Scavenger Hunt

FIND THE ANSWERS IN CHAPTER 8!

1. Who gets the king's ring?

2. Is it possible to revoke a law written in the king's name and sealed with the king's ring?

3. Where does the same שֹׁרֶשׁ (shoresh, word root) appear three times in a row?

4. Who wears royal clothing?

ג וַתּוֹסֶף אֶסְתֵּר וַתְּדַבֵּר לִפְנֵי הַמֶּלֶךְ וַתִּפֹּל לִפְנֵי רַגְלָיו וַתֵּבְךְּ וַתִּתְחַנֶּן־לוֹ לְהַעֲבִיר אֶת־רָעַת הָמָן הָאֲגָגִי וְאֵת מַחֲשַׁבְתּוֹ אֲשֶׁר חָשַׁב עַל־הַיְּהוּדִים: ד וַיּוֹשֶׁט הַמֶּלֶךְ לְאֶסְתֵּר אֵת שַׁרְבִט הַזָּהָב וַתָּקָם אֶסְתֵּר וַתַּעֲמֹד לִפְנֵי הַמֶּלֶךְ: ה וַתֹּאמֶר אִם־עַל־הַמֶּלֶךְ טוֹב וְאִם־מָצָאתִי חֵן לְפָנָיו וְכָשֵׁר הַדָּבָר לִפְנֵי הַמֶּלֶךְ וְטוֹבָה אֲנִי בְּעֵינָיו יִכָּתֵב לְהָשִׁיב אֶת־הַסְּפָרִים מַחֲשֶׁבֶת הָמָן בֶּן־הַמְּדָתָא הָאֲגָגִי אֲשֶׁר כָּתַב לְאַבֵּד אֶת־הַיְּהוּדִים אֲשֶׁר בְּכָל־מְדִינוֹת הַמֶּלֶךְ: ו כִּי אֵיכָכָה אוּכַל וְרָאִיתִי בָּרָעָה אֲשֶׁר־יִמְצָא אֶת־עַמִּי וְאֵיכָכָה אוּכַל וְרָאִיתִי בְּאָבְדַן מוֹלַדְתִּי:

פסוק ו - PASUK 6
This pasuk is read in the sad tune of Megillat Eikhah.

3 Esther spoke again to the king. She fell at his feet, crying and begging him to cancel Haman's evil plans for the Jews. 4 The king extended the golden scepter to Esther. She got up and stood before the king. 5 She said, "If it pleases Your Majesty, and if I have found compassion in your eyes, let it be written to bring back the scrolls with Haman's plan where he wrote about annihilating the Jews in all of the king's provinces. 6 For how can I bear to see the evil that will happen to my people?! How can I bear to see the annihilation of my family?!"

Tefillah

Pasuk 3
How many things does Esther do? (Read the pasuk carefully and count them!)

Esther speaks, falls down, cries, and begs. The Vilna Gaon explains that each of these things was very different from the others, and it was important for Esther to do them all:

אדרת אליהו

"וַתְּדַבֵּר... וַתִּפֹּל... וַתֵּבְךְּ"—הִיא מַחֲשָׁבָה דִּבּוּר מַעֲשֶׂה.

"וַתֵּבְךְּ" הוּא מַחֲשָׁבָה, כִּי אֵין בְּכִיָּה אֶלָּא בַּלֵּב.... וְהַכֹּל הוּא לְשׁוֹן תַּחֲנוּנִים, כְּמוֹ שֶׁנֶּאֱמַר "וַתִּתְחַנֶּן". וּכְמוֹ שֶׁאָמְרוּ (אבות ב:יג): אַל תַּעַשׂ תְּפִלָּתְךָ קֶבַע אֶלָּא רַחֲמִים וְתַחֲנוּנִים לִפְנֵי הַמָּקוֹם.

Vilna Gaon (Eastern Europe, 250 years ago)

"She spoke... she fell at his feet... she cried"—crying is thought, talking is speech, and falling down is action. We know that crying is thought because it comes from what's in our hearts.... All of them are ways to beg, as it says, "She begged him." As our Sages said: Do not make your prayers automatic, but rather pleas for compassion before God.

The Vilna Gaon believes that all things people do are either thoughts, words, or actions. So Esther does everything possible in order to save the Jewish people. She pours her heart out, she speaks up, and she bows to Ahashverosh. The Vilna Gaon connects this to the ways we pray before God. We don't just use our lips by saying the words, but we use our inner hearts and thoughts and we even try to use our bodies.

- If you're able to, what are some of the different ways you move your body during tefillah? Why would that be part of prayer?

- What are the thoughts or feelings we're supposed to have when we pray? Why isn't it good enough to just say the words without any thoughts or feelings?

- What does Esther's example teach us about helping others? Why is it important to try so many different things? What are some of the ways we can combine thoughts, actions, and words to help others?

זַ וַיֹּאמֶר הַמֶּלֶךְ אֲחַשְׁוֵרֹשׁ לְאֶסְתֵּר הַמַּלְכָּה וּלְמָרְדֳּכַי הַיְּהוּדִי הִנֵּה בֵית־הָמָן נָתַתִּי לְאֶסְתֵּר וְאֹתוֹ תָּלוּ עַל־הָעֵץ עַל אֲשֶׁר־שָׁלַח יָדוֹ בַּיְּהוּדִים: חַ וְאַתֶּם כִּתְבוּ עַל־הַיְּהוּדִים כַּטּוֹב בְּעֵינֵיכֶם בְּשֵׁם הַמֶּלֶךְ וְחִתְמוּ בְּטַבַּעַת הַמֶּלֶךְ כִּי־כְתָב אֲשֶׁר־נִכְתָּב בְּשֵׁם־הַמֶּלֶךְ וְנַחְתּוֹם בְּטַבַּעַת הַמֶּלֶךְ אֵין לְהָשִׁיב: טַ וַיִּקָּרְאוּ סֹפְרֵי־הַמֶּלֶךְ בָּעֵת־הַהִיא בַּחֹדֶשׁ הַשְּׁלִישִׁי הוּא־חֹדֶשׁ סִיוָן בִּשְׁלוֹשָׁה וְעֶשְׂרִים בּוֹ וַיִּכָּתֵב כְּכָל־אֲשֶׁר־צִוָּה מָרְדֳּכַי אֶל־הַיְּהוּדִים וְאֶל הָאֲחַשְׁדַּרְפְּנִים וְהַפַּחוֹת וְשָׂרֵי הַמְּדִינוֹת אֲשֶׁר מֵהֹדּוּ וְעַד־כּוּשׁ שֶׁבַע וְעֶשְׂרִים וּמֵאָה מְדִינָה מְדִינָה וּמְדִינָה כִּכְתָבָהּ וְעַם וָעָם כִּלְשֹׁנוֹ וְאֶל־הַיְּהוּדִים כִּכְתָבָם וְכִלְשׁוֹנָם:

7 King Ahashverosh said to Queen Esther and Mordekhai the Jew, "I've given Haman's household to Esther, and they hanged him on a post for trying to kill the Jews. 8 So you can write whatever you want about the Jews in the name of the king and sign it with the king's seal. For a law written in the name of the king and signed with the king's seal cannot be taken back." 9 So right then, on the 23rd of Sivan, the king's scribes were called, and everything Mordekhai commanded regarding the Jews was written. This was to be sent to all the governors from Hodu to Kush in all 127 provinces–to each one in its own writing, and to each people in their own language–and even to the Jews, in their own writing and language.

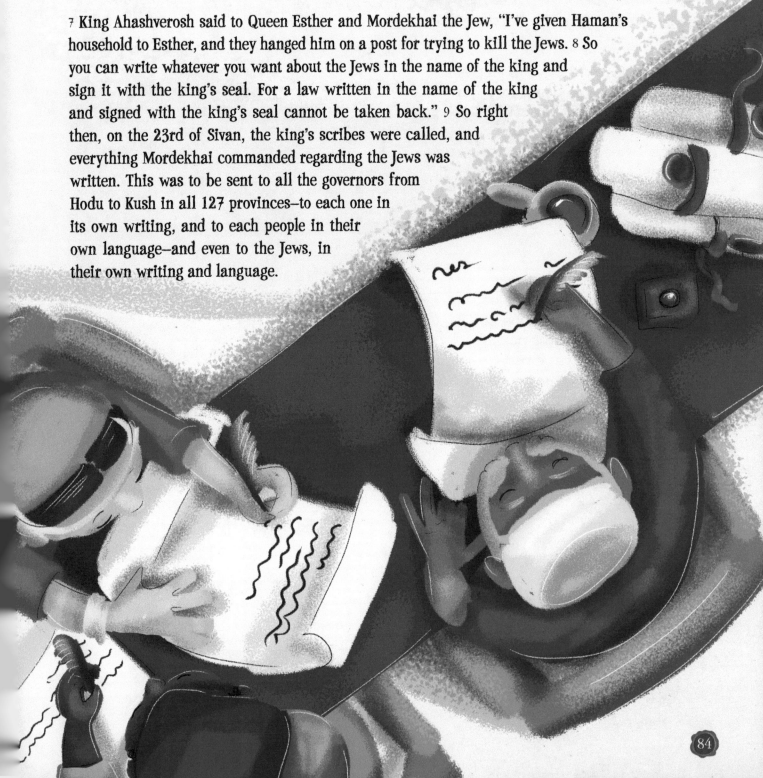

Pasuk 9
There are many words in the Megillah that aren't Hebrew!

The holiday of Purim is named after word from ancient Persia, pur, translated by the Megillah into the Hebrew גּוֹרָל (goral, lottery) (3:7). Here are some other words in the Megillah that come from Persian, some of which are now Hebrew words, too:

- אֲחַשְׁדַּרְפְּנִים (ahashdarpenim) = governors (3:12, 8:9, 9:3)

- פַּרְתְּמִים (partemim) = nobles (1:3, 6:9)

- דָּת (dat) = order, decree (4:8 and lots of other places)

- פִּתְגָם (pitgam) = decree, announcement (1:20)

- פַּתְשֶׁגֶן (patshegen) = copy (3:14, 4:8, 8:13)

- אֲחַשְׁתְּרָנִים (ahashteranim) = very fast horses (8:10, 8:14)

- What do you notice about these words? Are there any common themes that tie some of the words together?

- Languages have ways of sharing words with each other. Sometimes, Persian words can make their way into Hebrew (like dat), and sometimes Hebrew words make their way into other languages, like English! Are there Hebrew words you use in your life even when you're talking another language?

- TRY IT OUT! Look up the word "Megillah" in an English dictionary. What do you find there?

י וַיִּכְתֹּב בְּשֵׁם הַמֶּלֶךְ אֲחַשְׁוֵרֹשׁ וַיַּחְתֹּם בְּטַבַּעַת הַמֶּלֶךְ וַיִּשְׁלַח סְפָרִים בְּיַד הָרָצִים בַּסּוּסִים
רֹכְבֵי הָרֶכֶשׁ הָאֲחַשְׁתְּרָנִים בְּנֵי הָרַמָּכִים: יא אֲשֶׁר נָתַן הַמֶּלֶךְ לַיְּהוּדִים אֲשֶׁר

פסוק יא – PASUK 11
The reader first reads
לְהַשְׁמִיד לַהֲרֹג וּלְאַבֵּד,
followed immediately
by לְהַשְׁמִיד וְלַהֲרֹג וּלְאַבֵּד.

בְּכָל־עִיר וָעִיר לְהִקָּהֵל וְלַעֲמֹד עַל־נַפְשָׁם לְהַשְׁמִיד וְלַהֲרֹג וּלְאַבֵּד אֶת־כָּל־
חֵיל עַם וּמְדִינָה הַצָּרִים אֹתָם טַף וְנָשִׁים וּשְׁלָלָם לָבוֹז: יב בְּיוֹם אֶחָד בְּכָל־
מְדִינוֹת הַמֶּלֶךְ אֲחַשְׁוֵרוֹשׁ בִּשְׁלוֹשָׁה עָשָׂר לְחֹדֶשׁ שְׁנֵים־עָשָׂר הוּא־חֹדֶשׁ
אֲדָר: יג פַּתְשֶׁגֶן הַכְּתָב לְהִנָּתֵן דָּת בְּכָל־מְדִינָה וּמְדִינָה גָּלוּי לְכָל־הָעַמִּים וְלִהְיוֹת הַיְּהוּדִים
עֲתִידִים לַיּוֹם הַזֶּה לְהִנָּקֵם מֵאֹיְבֵיהֶם: יד הָרָצִים רֹכְבֵי הָרֶכֶשׁ הָאֲחַשְׁתְּרָנִים יָצְאוּ מְבֹהָלִים
וּדְחוּפִים בִּדְבַר הַמֶּלֶךְ וְהַדָּת נִתְּנָה בְּשׁוּשַׁן הַבִּירָה:

10 It was written in the name of King Ahashverosh and signed with the king's seal. And he sent scrolls out in the hands of all the messengers riding horses and speedy animals. 11 The scrolls said that the king gave the Jews in every city permission to gather and defend themselves, to destroy, kill, and annihilate the whole army of any people or province that threatens them or their children, and all of the enemies' possessions would be free for the taking. 12 There would be one day to do this in the entire kingdom: the 13th of Adar. 13 The decree was published to spread word of the law in all provinces, to all people, so that the Jews would be ready for that day to give their enemies a taste of their own medicine. 14 The messengers riding speedy animals rushed out with the king's decree, and the law was displayed in Shushan the capital.

Pasuk 10

What are these אֲחַשְׁתְּרָנִים בְּנֵי הָרַמָּכִים (ahashteranim benei ha-ramakhim)?

This phrase is a mouthful, and it's difficult to figure out because the main words are from Persian! (See page 85.) The Talmud even says that we do not know for certain what they could be (Megillah 18a).

Our פַּרְשָׁנִים (parshanim, commentators) have different ideas, though they all agree that these are fast animals that messengers could ride to deliver the new decree:

Rashi (France, 1,000 years ago) — רש״י

A type of camel that runs quickly.

מִין גְּמַלִּים הַמְמַהֲרִים לָרוּץ.

Rashbam (France, 950 years ago) — רשב״ם

These are the fastest running horses.

סוּסֵי הָרָצִים שֶׁהֵן קַלִּים לָרוּץ.

Ibn Ezra (Spain, 900 years ago) — אבן עזרא

Some say these are mules.

יֵשׁ אוֹמְרִים הַפְּרָדִים.

- Whatever these things were, it seems to have been really important to get the word out quickly. Why is that?

- What does the speed you use tell us about the importance of the thing you're doing? Can you think of examples of when it's better to do something slowly or when it's better to do a thing quickly?

טו וּמָרְדֳּכַי יָצָא מִלִּפְנֵי הַמֶּלֶךְ בִּלְבוּשׁ מַלְכוּת תְּכֵלֶת וָחוּר וַעֲטֶרֶת זָהָב גְּדוֹלָה וְתַכְרִיךְ בּוּץ וְאַרְגָּמָן וְהָעִיר שׁוּשָׁן צָהֲלָה וְשָׂמֵחָה: טז לַיְּהוּדִים הָיְתָה אוֹרָה וְשִׂמְחָה וְשָׂשֹׂן וִיקָר:

פסוקים טו-טז - PESUKIM 15–16
These two pesukim are first recited by the קָהָל (kahal, community) and then by the reader.

15 Mordekhai came away from the king wearing royal clothing embroidered with many colors, with a big golden crown, and a fancy robe. And the city of Shushan cheered and rejoiced! 16 The Jewish people had light, gladness, joy, and honor.

- Why is learning Torah or doing mitzvot a way of having more light in the world?

- Why is it important to know that the Torah is in our hearts? What does that teach us about ourselves? How can that be a source of joy even when things look dark?

- Do you recognize this pasuk from Havdalah, the prayer we say when Shabbat ends? How might Rashi or the Sefat Emet help us understand why the end of Shabbat, when it's dark, is a good time to say this pasuk?

Commentary

Pasuk 16
The Jews had light, gladness, joy, and honor!
What are each of these amazing things?

In the Gemara, Rav Yehudah explains that each of these words connects to a different mitzvah:

Talmud Bavli Megillah 16b	תלמוד בבלי מגילה דף טז עמוד ב
Rav Yehudah said: "Light"—this is Torah....	אָמַר רַב יְהוּדָה: "אוֹרָה"—זוֹ תּוֹרָה....
"Gladness"—this is holidays....	"שִׂמְחָה"—זֶה יוֹם טוֹב....
"Joy"—this is brit milah (circumcision)....	"שָׂשׂוֹן"—זוֹ מִילָה....
"Honor"—this is tefillin....	"וִיקָר"—אֵלּוּ תְּפִלִּין....

According to Rashi, Haman had prevented the Jewish people from observing these mitzvot, so being able to come back and do them again was a huge joy. Not being able to learn Torah is like being in a deep darkness. Being able to learn again is like having the light turned on for you!

The Sefat Emet takes this one step further.

שפת אמת, פורים יד

וְהָעִנְיָן הוּא כִּי כָּל הַמִּצְוֹת הֵם הַדְּרָכוֹת לָאָדָם לִמְצוֹא הָאוֹרוֹת הַמְיֻחָדִים לְכָל מִצְוָה וּמִצְוָה. וּבֶאֱמֶת הָעִקָּר כְּשֶׁהָאָדָם עַצְמוֹ מוֹצֵא אֵלֶּה הַהֶאָרוֹת בְּלִבּוֹ.... כְּמוֹ כֵן נִמְצָא בְּנֶפֶשׁ הָאָדָם עַצְמוֹ לְעוֹרֵר אֵלֶּה הַדְּבָרִים. וְזֶה שֶׁכָּתוּב "לַיְהוּדִים הָיְתָה אוֹרָה"—בְּעֶצֶם נַפְשׁוֹתָם.

Sefat Emet (Poland, 150 years ago)

The idea is that the mitzvot are paths for a person to find whatever special light comes along with each mitzvah. The truly important thing about mitzvot is for each person to find these lights in their hearts.... So each person can spark these lights within themselves. That is why the pasuk says, "The Jews had light"—they already had it, deep in their souls!

According to the Sefat Emet, the Torah is a part of you, deep in your soul and heart. Doing mitzvot is a way of bringing the light of the Torah that's inside you out into the world. That power is something we always have inside us, whether Haman prevents us from doing the mitzvot or not. So when the Megillah says that "the Jews had light," it's the truth. We had it in us all along.

יז וּבְכָל־מְדִינָה וּמְדִינָה וּבְכָל־עִיר וָעִיר מְקוֹם אֲשֶׁר דְּבַר־הַמֶּלֶךְ וְדָתוֹ מַגִּיעַ שִׂמְחָה וְשָׂשׂוֹן לַיְּהוּדִים מִשְׁתֶּה וְיוֹם טוֹב וְרַבִּים מֵעַמֵּי הָאָרֶץ מִתְיַהֲדִים כִּי־נָפַל פַּחַד־הַיְּהוּדִים עֲלֵיהֶם:

17 In every province and city—wherever the king's law arrived—there was joy, celebration, banqueting, and holidays for the Jews. And many people in the land made themselves appear Jewish because the fear of the Jews fell upon them.

מִדְרָשׁ
Midrash

Pesukim 16-17
How did we get to this happy ending?

Talmud Yerushalmi Berakhot 1:1, 2c

R. Hiyya Rabba said to R. Shimon bar Halafta: This is how Israel is saved; it starts out very small and grows and grows as it goes on. How do we know this? "When I sit in darkness, God is my light" (Mikhah 7:8).

So it was in the beginning of the story: "Mordekhai was in the king's court" (2:21).

After that: "Haman took the clothing and the horse and dressed Mordekhai" (6:11).

After that: "Mordekhai went back to the king's court" (6:12).

After that: "Mordekhai came away from the king wearing royal clothing" (8:15).

After that: "The Jewish people had light, gladness, joy, and honor" (8:16).

תלמוד ירושלמי ברכות א:א, דף ב טור ג

אָמַר רְבִּי חִיָּיא רַבָּא לְרְבִּי שִׁמְעוֹן בֶּן חֲלַפְתָּא בֵּירְבִּי כַּךְ הִיא גְּאֻלָּתָן שֶׁל יִשְׂרָאֵל בַּתְּחִילָה קִמְאָה קִמְאָה כָּל־מָה שֶׁהִיא הוֹלֶכֶת הִיא רָבָה וְהוֹלֶכֶת. מַאי טַעְמָא? "כִּי אֵשֵׁב בַּחֹשֶׁךְ ה' אוֹר לִי."

כֵּן בַּתְּחִילָה "וּמָרְדְּכַי יֹשֵׁב בְּשַׁעַר הַמֶּלֶךְ."

וְאַחַר כַּךְ "וַיִּקַּח הָמָן אֶת הַלְּבוּשׁ וְאֶת הַסּוּס."

וְאַחַר כַּךְ "וַיָּשָׁב מָרְדְּכַי אֶל שַׁעַר הַמֶּלֶךְ."

וְאַחַר כַּךְ "וּמָרְדְּכַי יָצָא מִלִּפְנֵי הַמֶּלֶךְ בִּלְבוּשׁ מַלְכוּת."

וְאַחַר כַּךְ "לַיְּהוּדִים הָיְתָה אוֹרָה וְשִׂמְחָה."

The Talmud teaches that salvation might take time and even come very slowly. In the times of greatest darkness, a small glimmer of light can grow larger and larger. R. Hiyya connects this idea to a pasuk in Sefer Mikhah that says that even when we sit in the dark, God is our light.

- What does it mean that God can be your light when it's dark? If it's dark, how can it also be light?

- How does this connect to what the Talmud teaches about the light the Jews experienced (page 89)?

- What other things take time to grow? Why do we sometimes have to work on things slowly instead of getting them all at once?

After the pasuk from Mikhah, the Talmud lists pesukim in Megillat Esther that show the idea that salvation starts slowly.

- How do these moments connect to each other? Do you see how they build upon each other? Why does the Talmud focus on Mordekhai's clothing and where he sits?

- Are there other moments that come to mind that demonstrate that the salvation grows through the Megillah?

וּבִשְׁנַיִם

עָשָׂר חֹדֶשׁ הוּא־חֹדֶשׁ אֲדָר בִּשְׁלוֹשָׁה עָשָׂר יוֹם בּוֹ אֲשֶׁר הִגִּיעַ דְּבַר־הַמֶּלֶךְ וְדָתוֹ לְהֵעָשׂוֹת בַּיּוֹם אֲשֶׁר שִׂבְּרוּ אֹיְבֵי הַיְּהוּדִים לִשְׁלוֹט בָּהֶם וְנַהֲפוֹךְ הוּא אֲשֶׁר יִשְׁלְטוּ הַיְּהוּדִים הֵמָּה בְּשֹׂנְאֵיהֶם:

1 The 13th of Adar was the day for the king's decree to be carried out. It was the day the enemies had hoped to rule over the Jews—but the opposite happened!—and the Jews ruled over their enemies.

שְׁאֵלוֹת
?
Scavenger Hunt

FIND THE ANSWERS IN CHAPTER 9!

1. How do you know it was opposite day?

2. Who was getting more and more famous?

3. There is one pasuk where four words are each repeated twice, one after the other. Can you find it?

4. How many times does the word פּוּרִים (Purim) appear in this chapter?

Pasuk 1

Instead of their enemies beating them, the Jews beat their enemies. In English, this is sometimes called "turning the tables." The Megillah describes this with the words וְנַהֲפוֹךְ הוּא (venahafokh hu, the opposite happened). But perhaps this phrase also hints at something else. Was there something venahafokh hu, opposite, about the way the Jews fought back against the people trying to hurt them?

Here are two features of the fighting that stand out.

 1 NO PLUNDERING

Haman and Ahashverosh's decree to annihilate the Jews stated that all of their possessions would be free for the taking (Esther 3:13). They wanted everyone to come grab all the Jews' stuff.

Ahashverosh then gave the same permission to the Jews to plunder the possessions of their enemies (8:11)! But in three separate pesukim in perek 9, we hear that the Jews did not do this. (Look it up! Esther 9:10, 9:15, 9:16.)

So why would the Jews not act in the same way that their enemies planned and just take their stuff? After all, they had the king's permission.

R. Shlomo Alkabetz explains that Mordekhai forbade the Jews from plundering because the fighting had to be strictly limited to self-defense:

R. Shlomo Alkabetz (Eretz Yisrael, 500 years ago)	**מנות הלוי אסתר ט:י**
Mordekhai and his court decided that the Jews should not take the plunder... to make sure Jews acting badly would not be tempted to fight innocent people out of their desire for money.... This was in order that the Jews should be seen	וְתַקָּנַת מָרְדְּכַי וּבֵית דִּינוֹ הָיְתָה... בַּעֲבוּר פְּרִיצֵי יִשְׂרָאֵל לֹא שָׁלְחוּ יְדֵיהֶם בְּמִי שֶׁלֹּא הִזִּיקָן בַּעֲבוּר חֶמְדַּת הַמָּמוֹן.... בַּעֲבוּר שֶׁיִּחְזְקוּ הַיְּהוּדִים בְּעֵינֵי הַמֶּלֶךְ וְהַשָּׂרִים אֲנָשִׁים צַדִּיקִים שׂוֹנְאֵי בֶצַע, שׂוֹנְאִים מָמוֹן בַּדִּין.

by the king and ministers as righteous people who hate greed, and who even hate taking money when the law is on their side.

<< **CONTINUED ON PAGE 95**

ב נִקְהֲל֣וּ הַיְּהוּדִ֣ים בְּעָרֵיהֶם֮ בְּכָל־מְדִינוֹת֮ הַמֶּ֣לֶךְ אֲחַשְׁוֵר֒וֹשׁ לִשְׁלֹ֣חַ יָ֗ד בִּמְבַקְשֵׁ֖י רָֽעָתָ֑ם וְאִישׁ֙ לֹא־עָמַ֣ד לִפְנֵיהֶ֔ם כִּֽי־נָפַ֥ל פַּחְדָּ֖ם עַל־כָּל־הָֽעַמִּֽים: ג וְכָל־שָׂרֵ֣י הַמְּדִינ֡וֹת וְהָאֲחַשְׁדַּרְפְּנִ֣ים וְהַפַּח֡וֹת וְעֹשֵׂ֣י הַמְּלָאכָ֣ה אֲשֶׁ֣ר לַמֶּלֶךְ֒ מְנַשְּׂאִ֖ים אֶת־הַיְּהוּדִ֑ים כִּֽי־נָפַ֥ל פַּֽחַד־מָרְדֳּכַ֖י עֲלֵיהֶֽם: ד כִּֽי־גָד֤וֹל מָרְדֳּכַי֙ בְּבֵ֣ית הַמֶּ֔לֶךְ וְשָׁמְע֖וֹ הוֹלֵ֣ךְ בְּכָל־הַמְּדִינ֑וֹת כִּֽי־הָאִ֥ישׁ מָרְדֳּכַ֖י הוֹלֵ֥ךְ וְגָדֽוֹל: ה וַיַּכּ֤וּ הַיְּהוּדִים֙ בְּכָל־אֹ֣יְבֵיהֶ֔ם מַכַּת־חֶ֥רֶב וְהֶ֖רֶג וְאַבְדָ֑ן וַיַּֽעֲשׂ֥וּ בְשֽׂנְאֵיהֶ֖ם כִּרְצוֹנָֽם:

PASUK 2 - ב פסוק
The reader first reads וְאִישׁ לֹא עָמַד בִּפְנֵיהֶם,
followed immediately by וְאִישׁ לֹא עָמַד לִפְנֵיהֶם.

2 The Jews gathered in their cities, in all the provinces of King Ahashverosh, to fight whoever wanted to do evil to them. No one stood in their way because everyone was afraid of them. 3 All of the king's ministers and governors supported the Jews because they were afraid of Mordekhai. 4 For Mordekhai had become important in the king's court, and his reputation had spread to all the provinces. Mordekhai was becoming more and more powerful. 5 The Jews struck their enemies with the sword, death, and annihilation. They did what they wanted with them.

R. Alkabetz says we can't celebrate when people fall, even if they tried to hurt us. The thing that makes us happy is being saved, not when people—as bad as they might be—are killed or hurt. He connects this to a midrash (Megillah 10b) about God telling the angels to stop celebrating while the Egyptians drowned in the Yam Suf.

- What is the difference between celebrating "being saved" and celebrating "beating enemies"? What different attitudes or character traits are shown in those different kinds of celebrations?

- What does this teach us about what's appropriate to celebrate and what's not? Even when violence is necessary for self-defense, how are we supposed to relate to that violence?

CONTINUED FROM PAGE 93 >>

- If Mordekhai allowed the Jews to take the plunder, why would that increase the risk that they would fight innocent people?

- What different messages did it send to not take their enemies' possessions? Why are these messages so important?

- What does R. Alkabetz teach us about how we should view other people's money, even if we have permission to take it? What should we learn from the Jews' behavior in this story?

 2 ## CELEBRATING PEACE, NOT WAR

Perek 9 emphasizes that the Jews celebrated the days of peace that came after the fighting ended, but did not celebrate the days on which there was fighting. (Look it up! 9:17, 9:18, 9:22.) This actually makes celebrating Purim really complicated because the Jews in Shushan kept fighting another day, which means they didn't rest until one day later (9:18). This is why Shushan Purim is a day later than Purim.

R. Alkabetz asks why we can't make things a lot simpler by just celebrating a different day:

R. Shlomo Alkabetz (Eretz Yisrael, 500 years ago)

מנות הלוי אסתר ט:ב

Why did they commemorate the time of peace and not the time of the miracle when the Jews broke their enemies and ruled over them, and when all the evil was turned upside down? That way there would be one day set for everyone to celebrate: the day of the miracle (when the fighting took place)!

וְלָמָּה עָשׂוּ זֵכֶר לִזְמַן הַמְּנוּחָה וְלֹא לִזְמַן הַנֵּס אֲשֶׁר הָיָה בַּיּוֹם אֲשֶׁר שָׁבְרוּ אֹיְבֵי הַיְּהוּדִים לִשְׁלוֹט בָּהֶם וְנַהֲפוֹךְ הוּא וְיִהְיֶה יוֹם אֶחָד קָבוּעַ לַכֹּל הוּא יוֹם הַנֵּס.

וְהַנִּרְאֶה לִי כִּי כִּי לִהְיוֹת מִדְּרָכָיו יִתְבָּרַךְ שֶׁאֵינוֹ שָׂמֵחַ בְּמַפַּלְתָּן שֶׁל רְשָׁעִים וּכְדִבְרֵי רַבִּי יוֹחָנָן (מגילה דף י עמוד ב)... אָמַר הַקָּדוֹשׁ בָּרוּךְ הוּא מַעֲשֵׂה יָדַי טוֹבְעִים בַּיָּם וְאַתֶּם אוֹמְרִים שִׁירָה?!... גַּם אֲנַחְנוּ נֵלֵךְ בִּדְרָכָיו וְנִשְׂמַח עַל הַמְּנוּחָה לֹא עַל הַהֲרִיגָה וְהַמַּפָּלָה.... יוֹרֶה כִּי עַל הַהַצָּלָתָם יָשִׂישׂוּ וְיִשְׂמְחוּ לֹא עַל זוּלַת זֶה.

It seems to me that it's to follow God's ways, and God does not rejoice in the downfall of the wicked. Like R. Yohanan said (Megillah 10b), "(At the Splitting of the Sea, the angels were not allowed to sing praises because) the Holy Blessed One said: My handiwork (the Egyptians) are drowning in the sea, and you want to sing before Me?!"... So we too are supposed to follow God's ways and only celebrate peace, not killing and destruction.... This teaches us that we can celebrate our own salvation, but nothing else.

פסוקים ו-י - 10–6 PESUKIM
The reader says the words from
איש at the end of pasuk 6 through
הָמָן in pasuk 10 all in one breath.

ז וּבְשׁוּשַׁן הַבִּירָה הָרְגוּ הַיְּהוּדִים וְאַבֵּד חֲמֵשׁ מֵאוֹת

אִישׁ:	ז וְאֵת
פַּרְשַׁנְדָּתָא	וְאֵת
דַּלְפוֹן	וְאֵת
אַסְפָּתָא:	ח וְאֵת
פּוֹרָתָא	וְאֵת
אֲדַלְיָא	וְאֵת
אֲרִידָתָא:	ט וְאֵת
פַּרְמַשְׁתָּא	וְאֵת
אֲרִיסַי	וְאֵת
אֲרִדַי	וְאֵת
וַיְזָתָא:	י עֲשֶׂרֶת

בְּנֵי הָמָן בֶּן־הַמְּדָתָא צֹרֵר הַיְּהוּדִים הָרָגוּ וּבַבִּזָּה לֹא שָׁלְחוּ אֶת־יָדָם: יא בַּיּוֹם הַהוּא בָּא מִסְפַּר הַהֲרוּגִים בְּשׁוּשַׁן הַבִּירָה לִפְנֵי הַמֶּלֶךְ: יב וַיֹּאמֶר הַמֶּלֶךְ לְאֶסְתֵּר הַמַּלְכָּה בְּשׁוּשַׁן הַבִּירָה הָרְגוּ הַיְּהוּדִים וְאַבֵּד חֲמֵשׁ מֵאוֹת אִישׁ וְאֵת עֲשֶׂרֶת בְּנֵי־הָמָן בִּשְׁאָר מְדִינוֹת הַמֶּלֶךְ מֶה עָשׂוּ וּמַה־שְּׁאֵלָתֵךְ וְיִנָּתֵן לָךְ וּמַה־בַּקָּשָׁתֵךְ עוֹד וְתֵעָשׂ: יג וַתֹּאמֶר אֶסְתֵּר אִם־עַל־הַמֶּלֶךְ טוֹב יִנָּתֵן גַּם־מָחָר לַיְּהוּדִים אֲשֶׁר בְּשׁוּשָׁן לַעֲשׂוֹת כְּדָת הַיּוֹם וְאֵת עֲשֶׂרֶת בְּנֵי־הָמָן יִתְלוּ עַל־הָעֵץ: יד וַיֹּאמֶר הַמֶּלֶךְ לְהֵעָשׂוֹת כֵּן וַתִּנָּתֵן דָּת בְּשׁוּשָׁן וְאֵת עֲשֶׂרֶת בְּנֵי־הָמָן תָּלוּ: טו וַיִּקָּהֲלוּ הַיְּהוּדִים אֲשֶׁר־בְּשׁוּשָׁן גַּם בְּיוֹם אַרְבָּעָה עָשָׂר לְחֹדֶשׁ אֲדָר וַיַּהַרְגוּ בְשׁוּשָׁן שְׁלֹשׁ מֵאוֹת אִישׁ וּבַבִּזָּה לֹא שָׁלְחוּ אֶת־יָדָם: טז וּשְׁאָר הַיְּהוּדִים אֲשֶׁר בִּמְדִינוֹת הַמֶּלֶךְ נִקְהֲלוּ וְעָמֹד עַל־נַפְשָׁם וְנוֹחַ מֵאֹיְבֵיהֶם וְהָרֹג בְּשֹׂנְאֵיהֶם חֲמִשָּׁה וְשִׁבְעִים אָלֶף וּבַבִּזָּה לֹא שָׁלְחוּ אֶת־יָדָם: יז בְּיוֹם־שְׁלוֹשָׁה עָשָׂר לְחֹדֶשׁ אֲדָר וְנוֹחַ בְּאַרְבָּעָה עָשָׂר בּוֹ וְעָשֹׂה אֹתוֹ יוֹם מִשְׁתֶּה וְשִׂמְחָה: יח וְהַיְּהוּדִים אֲשֶׁר־בְּשׁוּשָׁן נִקְהֲלוּ בִּשְׁלוֹשָׁה עָשָׂר בּוֹ וּבְאַרְבָּעָה עָשָׂר בּוֹ וְנוֹחַ בַּחֲמִשָּׁה עָשָׂר בּוֹ וְעָשֹׂה אֹתוֹ יוֹם מִשְׁתֶּה וְשִׂמְחָה: יט עַל־כֵּן הַיְּהוּדִים הַפְּרָזִים הַיֹּשְׁבִים בְּעָרֵי הַפְּרָזוֹת עֹשִׂים אֵת יוֹם אַרְבָּעָה עָשָׂר לְחֹדֶשׁ אֲדָר שִׂמְחָה וּמִשְׁתֶּה וְיוֹם טוֹב וּמִשְׁלֹחַ מָנוֹת אִישׁ לְרֵעֵהוּ: כ וַיִּכְתֹּב מָרְדֳּכַי אֶת־הַדְּבָרִים הָאֵלֶּה וַיִּשְׁלַח סְפָרִים אֶל־כָּל־הַיְּהוּדִים אֲשֶׁר בְּכָל־מְדִינוֹת הַמֶּלֶךְ אֲחַשְׁוֵרוֹשׁ הַקְּרוֹבִים וְהָרְחוֹקִים:

6 In Shushan the capital the Jews killed and annihilated 500

people,	7 and
Parshandata	and
Dalfon	and
Aspata	8 and
Porata	and
Adalya	and
Aridata	9 and
Parmashta	and
Arisai	and
Aridai	and
Vaizata,	10 the ten

sons of Haman, son of Hammedata, enemy of the Jews. They killed all those people, but they did not take any of their possessions. 11 That day, the number of deaths in Shushan was reported to the king. 12 The king said to Queen Esther, "In Shushan the capital the Jews killed and annihilated 500 people and the ten sons of Haman. And there might be more in other provinces. Do you have any more wishes and requests that have to be done?" 13 Esther said, "If it pleases Your Majesty, may the Jews in Shushan also have tomorrow to do what was done according to the law of today, and may the ten sons of Haman be hanged on a post?" 14 The king said that it should done. The law was given in Shushan, and the ten sons of Haman were hanged. 15 The Jews gathered in Shushan also on the 14th of Adar. They killed 300 people in Shushan, but they did not take any of their possessions. 16 The rest of the Jews in the king's provinces gathered and defended themselves, and then were at peace from their enemies. They killed 75,000 of their enemies, but they did not take any of their possessions. 17 That was on the 13th day of Adar. They were at peace on the 14th day, and that was the day they made for banqueting and joy. 18 But the Jews in Shushan gathered to fight on the 13th and 14th of Adar, and were only at peace on the 15th. So it was the 15th that was made into the day of banqueting and joy in Shushan. 19 That's why Jews living all around, outside of Shushan, celebrate a holiday on the 14th of Adar with joy and parties, sending *mishloah manot* (food packages) to their friends. 20 Mordekhai wrote all this down and sent scrolls to the Jews in King Ahashverosh's provinces, near and far.

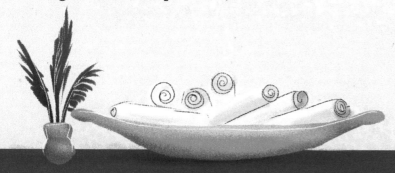

כא לְקַיֵּם֙ עֲלֵיהֶ֔ם לִהְי֣וֹת עֹשִׂ֗ים אֵ֠ת י֣וֹם אַרְבָּעָ֤ה עָשָׂר֙ לְחֹ֣דֶשׁ אֲדָ֔ר וְאֵ֛ת יֽוֹם־חֲמִשָּׁ֥ה עָשָׂ֖ר בּ֑וֹ בְּכׇל־שָׁנָ֖ה וְשָׁנָֽה: כב כַּיָּמִ֗ים אֲשֶׁר־נָ֨חוּ בָהֶ֤ם הַיְּהוּדִים֙ מֵאֹ֣יְבֵיהֶ֔ם וְהַחֹ֗דֶשׁ אֲשֶׁר֩ נֶהְפַּ֨ךְ לָהֶ֤ם מִיָּגוֹן֙ לְשִׂמְחָ֔ה וּמֵאֵ֖בֶל לְי֣וֹם ט֑וֹב לַעֲשׂ֣וֹת אוֹתָ֗ם יְמֵי֙ מִשְׁתֶּ֣ה וְשִׂמְחָ֔ה וּמִשְׁלֹ֤חַ מָנוֹת֙ אִ֣ישׁ לְרֵעֵ֔הוּ וּמַתָּנ֖וֹת לָאֶבְיוֹנִֽים:

21 He wanted them to accept upon themselves to observe these days of the 14th and 15th of Adar every year, 22 just like the two days of Adar in this story, when the Jews were at peace from their enemies and when their sorrow became joy and their mourning became a holiday. He wanted them to make these into days of feasting and joy, sending mishloah manot to friends, and *matanot la-evyonim* (gifts to the poor).

③ GIFTS TO PEOPLE WHO ARE POOR

There is no better way to spread our joy than to give מַתָּנוֹת לָאֶבְיוֹנִים (matanot la-evyonim), money or food to those who need it most (Mishneh Torah Hilkhot Megillah 2:17). The core of matanot la-evyonim is to give one gift, normally money (but it could also be food), to two different people. This mitzvah is the highest priority. It's better to spend more money on matanot la-evyonim than on the seudah and mishloah manot combined (Mishnah Berurah 694:3)!

You have to be sure that the money will be given directly to people in need on the day of Purim and no later.

④ READING THE MEGILLAH

The source for this mitzvah comes later in our perek, in pasuk 28: וְהַיָּמִים הָאֵלֶּה נִזְכָּרִים וְנַעֲשִׂים (these days are remembered and observed). Reading the Megillah out loud from a scroll is how we do this "remembering." The mitzvah is to either read Megillat Esther yourself or hear someone else read it. This is done twice, once at night and once in the morning (Mishneh Torah Hilkhot Megillah 1:1–2).

It's very important to hear every single word of the Megillah, even the name of a certain wicked person that we try to block out with noise!

הֲלָכָה
Halakhah

Three of the mitzvot come from pasuk 22:

1 FEASTING AND JOY

The "feasting and joy" on Purim is called the Purim סְעוּדָה (seudah, meal). Almost everyone agrees that it should be eaten during the day, not the night before, and should be a fun occasion with friends and family (Shulhan Arukh Orah Hayyim 695:1).

2 SENDING FOOD

This is called מִשְׁלוֹחַ מָנוֹת (mishloah manot). The core of this mitzvah is to give two separate pieces of food to another Jew on the day of Purim (Shulhan Arukh Orah Hayyim 695:4). It can actually be two portions of the same food, as long as they taste a little different from each other. The point of mishloah manot is to make sure everyone has food for their seudah (Terumat Hadeshen 111). So whatever you give should be ready-to-eat.

כג וְקִבֵּל הַיְּהוּדִים אֵת אֲשֶׁר־הֵחֵלּוּ לַעֲשׂוֹת וְאֵת אֲשֶׁר־כָּתַב מָרְדֳּכַי אֲלֵיהֶם: כד כִּי הָמָן בֶּן־הַמְּדָתָא הָאֲגָגִי צֹרֵר כָּל־הַיְּהוּדִים חָשַׁב עַל־הַיְּהוּדִים לְאַבְּדָם וְהִפִּיל פּוּר הוּא הַגּוֹרָל לְהֻמָּם וּלְאַבְּדָם: כה וּבְבֹאָהּ לִפְנֵי הַמֶּלֶךְ אָמַר עִם־הַסֵּפֶר יָשׁוּב מַחֲשַׁבְתּוֹ הָרָעָה אֲשֶׁר־חָשַׁב עַל־הַיְּהוּדִים עַל־רֹאשׁוֹ וְתָלוּ אֹתוֹ וְאֶת־בָּנָיו עַל־הָעֵץ: כו עַל־כֵּן קָרְאוּ לַיָּמִים הָאֵלֶּה פוּרִים עַל־שֵׁם הַפּוּר עַל־כֵּן עַל־כָּל־דִּבְרֵי הָאִגֶּרֶת הַזֹּאת וּמָה־רָאוּ עַל־כָּכָה וּמָה הִגִּיעַ אֲלֵיהֶם: כז קִיְּמוּ וְקִבְּלוּ הַיְּהוּדִים עֲלֵיהֶם וְעַל־זַרְעָם וְעַל כָּל־הַנִּלְוִים עֲלֵיהֶם וְלֹא יַעֲבוֹר לִהְיוֹת עֹשִׂים אֵת שְׁנֵי הַיָּמִים הָאֵלֶּה כִּכְתָבָם וְכִזְמַנָּם בְּכָל־שָׁנָה וְשָׁנָה:

פסוק כו - PASUK 26
The reader lifts up the Megillah scroll when saying the words הָאִגֶּרֶת הַזֹּאת (this Megillah), and then again for the words אִגֶרֶת הַפּוּרִים הַזֹּאת in pasuk 29.

23 The Jews continued the celebrations they had already started, accepting everything Mordekhai wrote to them. 24 For Haman, son of Hammedata the Agagi, enemy of all the Jews, planned to annihilate them. He made a *pur*–that is the raffle–to terrorize and annihilate them. 25 But when Esther went to the king on behalf of the Jews, he said in writing to overturn the evil plot the enemy intended against the Jews, and that wicked man and his sons were hanged on a post. 26 That's why these days are called Purim, and this is why we have this Megillah! It's because of the *pur* and the story of what they saw and what happened to them. 27 The Jews upheld and accepted upon themselves and their descendants, and anyone who might join them–with no take-backs!–to observe these two days, at the right time and as they were written, every year.

מִדְרָשׁ Midrash

Pasuk 27
There's something strange about the order of the actions here. How can קִיְּמוּ (kiyemu, they upheld) happen before קִבְּלוּ (kibelu, they accepted)? It makes sense to first accept a mitzvah and then do it, not the other way around!

Talmud Bavli Shabbat 88a

"And they stood at the bottom of the mountain" (Shemot 19:17)—Rav Avdimi bar Hama bar Hasa said: This teaches that the Holy Blessed One held the mountain above their heads like a barrel, and said to them: If you accept the Torah, good. But if not, there will be your burial place....

Rava said: Even if the Jews were forced to accept the Torah at Har Sinai, they accepted the Torah again of their own free will in the time of Ahashverosh, as it is written: "The Jews upheld and accepted." This means that they upheld what they had already accepted at Har Sinai.

תלמוד בבלי שבת דף פח עמוד א

"וַיִּתְיַצְּבוּ בְּתַחְתִּית הָהָר"—אָמַר רַב אַבְדִּימִי בַּר חָמָא בַּר חַסָּא: מְלַמֵּד שֶׁכָּפָה הַקָּדוֹשׁ בָּרוּךְ הוּא עֲלֵיהֶם אֶת הָהָר כְּגִיגִית, וְאָמַר לָהֶם: אִם אַתֶּם מְקַבְּלִים הַתּוֹרָה מוּטָב, וְאִם לָאו, שָׁם תְּהֵא קְבוּרַתְכֶם....

אָמַר רָבָא: אַף עַל פִּי כֵן הֲדוּר קַבְּלוּהָ בִּימֵי אֲחַשְׁוֵרוֹשׁ, דִּכְתִיב: "קִיְּמוּ וְקִבְּלוּ הַיְּהוּדִים"— קִיְּמוּ מַה שֶׁקִּבְּלוּ כְּבָר.

According to this midrash, Benei Yisrael didn't have a choice when they received the Torah at Har Sinai. This explains why, in Shemot, it sounds like they were standing "underneath" the mountain—it's like it was being held over their heads. They were forced into it!

Rava thinks that this all got corrected in the Purim story. The words kiyemu ve-kibelu teach us that the Jews finally accepted the Torah of their own free will.

• Why is it important to accept the Torah out of free will? In what ways is Megillat Esther a story about Jewish people accepting the Torah? How is it about making an active choice to be Jewish?

כה וְהַיָּמִים הָאֵ֫לֶּה נִזְכָּרִים וְנַעֲשִׂים בְּכָל־דּוֹר וָדוֹר מִשְׁפָּחָה מִשְׁפָּחָה מְדִינָה וּמְדִינָה וְעִיר וָעִיר
וִימֵי הַפּוּרִים הָאֵ֫לֶּה לֹא יַעַבְרוּ מִתּוֹךְ הַיְּהוּדִים וְזִכְרָם לֹא־יָסוּף מִזַּרְעָם: כט וַתִּכְתֹּב אֶסְתֵּר
הַמַּלְכָּה בַת־אֲבִיחַ֫יִל וּמָרְדֳּכַ֫י הַיְּהוּדִי אֶת־כָּל־תֹּקֶף לְקַיֵּם אֵת אִגֶּרֶת הַפֻּרִים הַזֹּאת הַשֵּׁנִית:
ל וַיִּשְׁלַח סְפָרִים אֶל־כָּל־הַיְּהוּדִים אֶל־שֶׁבַע וְעֶשְׂרִים וּמֵאָה מְדִינָה מַלְכוּת אֲחַשְׁוֵרוֹשׁ דִּבְרֵי
שָׁלוֹם וֶאֱמֶת: לא לְקַיֵּם אֶת־יְמֵי הַפֻּרִים הָאֵ֫לֶּה בִּזְמַנֵּיהֶם כַּאֲשֶׁר קִיַּם עֲלֵיהֶם מָרְדֳּכַ֫י הַיְּהוּדִי
וְאֶסְתֵּר הַמַּלְכָּה וְכַאֲשֶׁר קִיְּמוּ עַל־נַפְשָׁם וְעַל־זַרְעָם דִּבְרֵי הַצֹּמוֹת וְזַעֲקָתָם: לב וּמַאֲמַר
אֶסְתֵּר קִיַּם דִּבְרֵי הַפֻּרִים הָאֵ֫לֶּה וְנִכְתָּב בַּסֵּפֶר:

28 These days are remembered and observed every generation by every family in every province
and every city. The days of Purim will never fade away from the Jewish people, and their children
will remember them forever. 29 Together with Mordekhai the Jew, Queen Esther, daughter of
Avihayil, also wrote something–this Purim Megillah!–about the greatness of this story and
the importance of celebrating it. 30 They sent scrolls to all the Jews, to all 127 provinces in
Ahashverosh's kingdom, with words of peace and truth 31 that they should celebrate these days of
Purim each year on the right dates–just as Mordekhai the Jew and Queen Esther had done before,
and just as the Jews and their children had accepted upon themselves–together with other times
of fasting and praying. 32 Esther's word is what made Purim official, and it was all written in
a scroll.

Pesukim 28-32
These pesukim tell us how the Megillah became accepted by the Jewish people, eventually becoming part of the Tanakh (Bible).

In perek 5 (page 55), though, we learned that God's name does not appear in the Megillah. So how did it end up getting included in the Tanakh at all?

Here's one answer from our Rabbis:

Talmud Bavli Megillah 7a	**תלמוד בבלי מגילה דף ז עמוד א**

Rav, Rav Hanina, R. Yohanan (or R. Yonatan), and Rav Haviva taught it in this way:

רַב וְרַב חֲנִינָא וְרַבִּי יוֹחָנָן וְרַב חֲבִיבָא מַתְנוּ. בְּכוּלֵּיהּ סֵדֶר מוֹעֵד כָּל כִּי הַאי זוּגָא חַלּוֹפֵי רַבִּי יוֹחָנָן וּמְעַיֵּיל רַבִּי יוֹנָתָן. שָׁלְחָה לָהֶם אֶסְתֵּר לַחֲכָמִים: כִּתְבוּנִי לְדוֹרוֹת.

Esther sent a message to the Sages, "Write me for generations (in Tanakh)!"

They sent a message to her, "'Did I not write for you three times!?' (Mishlei 22:20)—three times and not four!"

שָׁלְחוּ לָהּ: "הֲלֹא כָתַבְתִּי לְךָ שָׁלִישִׁים" (משלי כב:כ)— שָׁלִישִׁים וְלֹא רִבֵּעִים.

But then they found it written in the Torah, "Write this, a remembrance in a scroll" (Shemot 17:14). "Write this"—what is written about Amalek in Shemot and in Devarim; "a remembrance"—what is written about Amalek in Shmuel Alef; "in a scroll"—what is written in the Megillah.

עַד שֶׁמָּצְאוּ לוֹ מִקְרָא כָּתוּב בַּתּוֹרָה: "כְּתֹב זֹאת זִכָּרוֹן בַּסֵּפֶר" (שמות יז:יד). "כְּתֹב זֹאת"—מַה שֶּׁכָּתוּב כָּאן וּבְמִשְׁנֵה תוֹרָה. "זִכָּרוֹן"—מַה שֶּׁכָּתוּב בַּנְּבִיאִים, "בַּסֵּפֶר"—מַה שֶּׁכָּתוּב בַּמְּגִלָּה.

As we saw in perek 2 (page 19), the Purim story reflects an age-old conflict between Amalek and the Jewish people. This conflict comes up three times in the rest of the Tanakh (Shemot 17, Devarim 25, and Shmuel Alef 15). The Sages weren't sure if it really had to be told a fourth time. But in the end, they found a pasuk that seemed to predict that they would need to tell this story again when it would appear in a Megillah, and that's how Esther ended up kept forever in the Tanakh!

- Why was it so important to Esther that the story be recorded in Tanakh? When you read the Purim story, and when you think about your life, why is it so important to have things written down? What happens to stories when they're not?

- Why do we need to tell this story of Amalek four different times? What's the benefit of telling the same story over and over in different ways?

- What makes this particular story of Amalek different from all the others? What does it add?

הַמֶּלֶךְ אֲחַשְׁוֵרוֹשׁ מַס עַל־הָאָרֶץ וְאִיֵּי הַיָּם: ב וְכָל־מַעֲשֵׂה תָקְפּוֹ
וּגְבוּרָתוֹ וּפָרָשַׁת גְּדֻלַּת מָרְדֳּכַי אֲשֶׁר גִּדְּלוֹ הַמֶּלֶךְ הֲלוֹא־הֵם כְּתוּבִים
עַל־סֵפֶר דִּבְרֵי הַיָּמִים לְמַלְכֵי מָדַי וּפָרָס: ג כִּי מָרְדֳּכַי הַיְּהוּדִי
מִשְׁנֶה לַמֶּלֶךְ אֲחַשְׁוֵרוֹשׁ וְגָדוֹל לַיְּהוּדִים וְרָצוּי לְרֹב אֶחָיו ...

PASUK 3 - פסוק ג
This pasuk is first recited by the קָהָל (kahal,
community) and then by the reader.

1 King Ahashverosh made a tax for the land and the sea islands. 2 All his deeds of strength and power, and the story of Mordekhai's greatness–whom the king promoted–are they not written down in the History Book of the Kings of Madai and Persia?! 3 For Mordekhai the Jew became second-in-command to King Ahashverosh. He continued to be really important to the Jews and was liked by most of his people....

שְׁאֵלוֹת

? Scavenger Hunt

FIND THE ANSWERS IN CHAPTER 10!

1. What new place do we hear about for the first time?

2. What book is mentioned?

3. What was Mordekhai's new role?

Pasuk 3
At the very end of the Megillah, we hear that Mordekhai was liked by רֹב אֶחָיו (rov ehav). What does this mean?

Here's one possibility:

Rashbam (France, 950 years ago)

This simply means "all" his people.

רשב״ם

הוּא הַדִּין לְכָל אֶחָיו, לְפִי פְּשׁוּטוֹ.

According to Rashbam, rov here means something like הַרְבֵּה (harbei, many). Mordekhai was liked by everyone—so many people!

- Why is the Megillah trying to teach this? What's the lesson we're supposed to learn?

The Talmud records another opinion:

Talmud Bavli Megillah 16b

"Among most of his brothers"—but not "all" of his brothers. This teaches that some of the Sanhedrin separated from Mordekhai.

תלמוד בבלי מגילה דף טז עמוד ב

"לְרֹב אֶחָיו"—וְלֹא כָּל אֶחָיו. מְלַמֵּד שֶׁפֵּירְשׁוּ מִמֶּנּוּ מִקְצָת סַנְהֶדְרִין.

According to this interpretation, Mordekhai was a member of the Sanhedrin, the ancient council made up at that time of 70 Sages and elders. These other Sages were Mordekhai's "brothers." The word rov teaches us that when Mordekhai replaced Haman as King Ahashverosh's second-in-command, a small portion of the Sanhedrin stopped being friends with Mordekhai.

- Why do you think some members of the Sanhedrin might have been nervous about Mordekhai getting too close to Ahashverosh? What does this say about their attitude to Ahashverosh or to becoming a powerful member of his court?

- Maharitz (Eretz Yisrael, 400 years ago) wonders why it's so hard to please people sometimes. Mordekhai "spent his days striving for goodness and peace for his nation and all their children" (10:3), and yet he still couldn't get everyone to like him! Do you ever feel that way? Why do you think some people couldn't appreciate Mordekhai's work on their behalf? How can we use this to improve our own ability to appreciate others?

... דָּרַשׁ טוֹב לְעַמּוֹ וְדֹבֵר שָׁלוֹם לְכָל-זַרְעוֹ:

... He spent his days striving for goodness and peace for his nation and all their children.

- R. Shimshon Hayyim Nahmani (Italy, 300 years ago) says this is why we do mitzvot like matanot la-evyonim and mishloah manot after hearing the Megillah. These are designed to create more peace!

- **TRY IT OUT!** Think of ways to create more peace for others. What will you do?

Mazal tov!

You've learned all the way through Megillat Esther!

Let's conclude the same way that the Megillah, the Mishnah, and the Vilna Gaon conclude, with a berakhah for peace: May we have peace and blessings for us and for all of Israel forever. Amen!

Pasuk 3
What does it mean that Mordekhai spent his days striving for goodness and peace? And why is peace the very last idea in the Megillah?

Vilna Gaon (Lithuania, 250 years ago)   אדרת אליהו

He (Mordekhai) would benefit all nations.... He would speak peacefully with everybody. And because of that they would treat his children with peace forever.

שֶׁהָיָה מֵטִיב עִם כָּל הָאֻמּוֹת.... שֶׁהָיָה דּוֹבֵר שָׁלוֹם עִם הַכֹּל, וּמִזֶּה הִגִּיעַ שָׁלוֹם לְכָל זַרְעוֹ עַד עוֹלָם. וְשָׁלוֹם וּבְרָכָה יִהְיֶה לָנוּ וּלְכָל יִשְׂרָאֵל עַד הָעוֹלָם. אָמֵן.

May we have peace and blessings for us and for all of Israel forever. Amen!

The Vilna Gaon explains that Mordekhai spoke kindly to all people, and this created peace for the Jews. After a long story about people wanting to kill the Jewish people, it's nice to end off with a thought that Mordekhai was able to create peace for all people!

- It's easy to think that you need to be selfish if you want good things for yourself. But Mordekhai was able to show that by being kind to all people, he created peace for his own people. Why does it work that way? How so?

- What does this teach us about the power of speech? How does speaking kindly to all people create more peace?

Do you see how the Vilna Gaon ends his comment? This is the end of the Megillah, and also the end of his commentary on the Megillah. He notices that the last point of the Megillah is about creating peace. This is also how the very last mishnah at the end of the Talmud concludes:

Mishnah Okatzin 3:12   משנה עוקצין ג:יב

R. Shimon ben Halafta said: The Holy Blessed One found no vessel that could contain berakhah (blessing) for Israel except for peace, as it is written: "God will give strength to God's people; God will bless God's people with peace" (Tehillim 29:11).

אָמַר רַבִּי שִׁמְעוֹן בֶּן חֲלַפְתָּא, לֹא מָצָא הַקָּדוֹשׁ בָּרוּךְ הוּא כְּלִי מַחֲזִיק בְּרָכָה לְיִשְׂרָאֵל אֶלָּא הַשָּׁלוֹם, שֶׁנֶּאֱמַר (תהלים כט:יא): ה' עֹז לְעַמּוֹ יִתֵּן ה' יְבָרֵךְ אֶת עַמּוֹ בַשָּׁלוֹם.

- Why do you think it's so important to end with a berakhah for peace? Why is that such a good way to end a book?

Mordekhai prayed when he heard Haman's decree

ב When Mordekhai saw that a time of anger had started, and Haman's plans were spreading in Shushan,

ל He dressed in rags and tied himself to his mourning, he decreed a fast and sat in ashes.

כִּרְאוֹת מָרְדְּכַי כִּי יָצָא קֶצֶף, וְדָתֵי הָמָן נִתְּנוּ בְּשׁוּשָׁן.
לָבֵשׁ שַׂק וְקָשַׁר מִסְפֵּד, וְגָזַר צוֹם וַיֵּשֶׁב עַל הָאֵפֶר.

Esther defeated Haman

מ Who would stand up to gain forgiveness for the mistakes and apologize for the sins of our ancestors?

נ A flower blossomed from a lulav (palm) branch! Hadassah (Esther) arose to wake people up.

ס Her servants rushed Haman to make him drink the poison of serpents.

מִי זֶה יַעֲמֹד לְכַפֵּר שְׁגָגָה, וְלִמְחֹל חַטֵּאת עֲוֹן אֲבוֹתֵינוּ.
נֵץ פָּרַח מִלּוּלָב, הֵן הֲדַסָּה עָמְדָה לְעוֹרֵר יְשֵׁנִים.
סָרִיסֶיהָ הִבְהִילוּ לְהָמָן, לְהַשְׁקוֹתוֹ יֵין חֲמַת תַּנִּינִים.

Haman got what he deserved

ע His wealth stood him up, but his wickedness made him fall; he made a post for Mordekhai, but he was hanged on it himself.

עָמַד בְּעָשְׁרוֹ וְנָפַל בְּרִשְׁעוֹ, עָשָׂה לוֹ עֵץ וְנִתְלָה עָלָיו.

The Jews celebrated

פ The Jewish people all over the world opened their mouths to thank God, for Haman's lottery was turned into our luck.

צ Righteous Mordekhai was rescued from wicked Haman's hand, the enemy was killed instead of him.

ק The Jews accepted on themselves to celebrate Purim and to rejoice every year.

פִּיהֶם פָּתְחוּ כָּל יוֹשְׁבֵי תֵבֵל, כִּי פוּר הָמָן נֶהְפַּךְ לְפוּרֵנוּ.
צַדִּיק נֶחֱלַץ מִיַּד רָשָׁע, אוֹיֵב נִתַּן תַּחַת נַפְשׁוֹ.
קִימוּ עֲלֵיהֶם לַעֲשׂוֹת פּוּרִים, וְלִשְׂמֹחַ בְּכָל שָׁנָה וְשָׁנָה.

Let's all thank God!

ר You (God) saw the prayer of Mordekhai and Esther, You hanged Haman and his sons on the post.

רָאִיתָ אֶת תְּפִלַּת מָרְדְּכַי וְאֶסְתֵּר, הָמָן וּבָנָיו עַל הָעֵץ תָּלִיתָ.

ש The rose of Yaakov (the nation of Israel) rejoiced and was glad when they saw together Mordekhai's royal blue clothes.

ת You have always been their salvation and their hope in every generation.

שׁוֹשַׁנַּת יַעֲקֹב צָהֲלָה וְשָׂמֵחָה, בִּרְאוֹתָם יַחַד תְּכֵלֶת מָרְדְּכָי.
תְּשׁוּעָתָם הָיִיתָ לָנֶצַח, וְתִקְוָתָם בְּכָל דּוֹר וָדוֹר.

Let it be known that all those who hope in You will never be ashamed, and anyone who trusts in You will not be disgraced.

Cursed is Haman who sought to destroy me; blessed is Mordekhai the Jew.

Cursed is Zeresh, wife of the bully; blessed is Esther, who stood up for me.

Cursed are all the wicked; blessed are all the righteous, and may Harvonah also be remembered for good!

לְהוֹדִיעַ שֶׁכָּל קֹוֶיךָ לֹא יֵבֹשׁוּ, וְלֹא יִכָּלְמוּ לָנֶצַח כָּל הַחוֹסִים בָּךְ.
אָרוּר הָמָן אֲשֶׁר בִּקֵּשׁ לְאַבְּדִי, בָּרוּךְ מָרְדְּכַי הַיְּהוּדִי.
אֲרוּרָה זֶרֶשׁ אֵשֶׁת מַפְחִידִי, בְּרוּכָה אֶסְתֵּר בַּעֲדִי.
אֲרוּרִים כָּל הָרְשָׁעִים, בְּרוּכִים כָּל הַצַּדִּיקִים, וְגַם חַרְבוֹנָה זָכוּר לַטּוֹב!

בְּרָכוֹת
Blessings

> After finishing the Megillah, the reader recites this בְּרָכָה (berakhah, blessing):

Blessed are You, God our Lord, Ruler of the world, Who fights our battles, judges our cases, exacts revenge on our behalf, pays back our enemies, and saves us from trouble. Blessed are You, God, Who saves the people of Israel from those who cause them trouble, the God Who brings salvation.	בָּרוּךְ אַתָּה יהוה אֱלֹהֵינוּ מֶלֶךְ הָעוֹלָם הָרָב אֶת רִיבֵנוּ וְהַדָּן אֶת דִּינֵנוּ וְהַנּוֹקֵם אֶת נִקְמָתֵנוּ וְהַמְשַׁלֵּם גְּמוּל לְכָל אוֹיְבֵי נַפְשֵׁנוּ וְהַנִּפְרָע לָנוּ מִצָּרֵינוּ. בָּרוּךְ אַתָּה יהוה הַנִּפְרָע לְעַמּוֹ יִשְׂרָאֵל מִכָּל צָרֵיהֶם הָאֵל הַמּוֹשִׁיעַ.

> On Purim night, we recite the poem below.
>
> On Purim day, we sing just the final lines of the poem, beginning with the words שׁוֹשַׁנַּת יַעֲקֹב (Shoshannat Yaakov, The rose of Yaakov).

Introduction – God foiled Haman's plans

א God stopped the plans of the nations and canceled the plots of the sneaky people.

אֲשֶׁר הֵנִיא עֲצַת גּוֹיִם,
וַיָּפֶר מַחְשְׁבוֹת עֲרוּמִים.

ב When a wicked person rose against us, an evil descendant of Amalek.

בְּקוּם עָלֵינוּ אָדָם רָשָׁע,
נֵצֶר זָדוֹן מִזֶּרַע עֲמָלֵק.

Haman fell into his own trap

ג Haman bragged about his wealth and dug himself a hole, and his own greatness trapped him.

גָּאָה בְּעָשְׁרוֹ וְכָרָה לוֹ בּוֹר,
וּגְדֻלָּתוֹ יָקְשָׁה לּוֹ לָכֶד.

ד He imagined to himself that he would trap others, but he was trapped himself; he tried to destroy others, but he got destroyed right away.

דִּמָּה בְנַפְשׁוֹ לִלְכֹּד וְנִלְכַּד,
בִּקֵּשׁ לְהַשְׁמִיד וְנִשְׁמַד מְהֵרָה.

ה Haman showed the hatred of his ancestors going back to Esav; he brought the old hatred between Esav and Yaakov to their children.

הָמָן הוֹדִיעַ אֵיבַת אֲבוֹתָיו,
וְעוֹרֵר שִׂנְאַת אַחִים לַבָּנִים.

ו He didn't remember Shaul's mercy that, in his compassion for Agag, let Haman be born.

וְלֹא זָכַר רַחֲמֵי שָׁאוּל, כִּי
בְחֶמְלָתוֹ עַל אֲגָג נוֹלַד אוֹיֵב.

ז Wicked Haman schemed to cut down righteous Mordekhai, but the impure one was trapped in the hands of the pure one.

זָמַם רָשָׁע לְהַכְרִית צַדִּיק,
וְנִלְכַּד טָמֵא בִּידֵי טָהוֹר.

ח The kindness of Mordekhai and Esther overcame the mistake of Shaul, while Haman added his own sins to the sins of Esav.

חֶסֶד גָּבַר עַל שִׁגְגַת אָב,
וְרָשָׁע הוֹסִיף חֵטְא עַל חֲטָאָיו.

ט Haman hid his wicked thoughts in his heart, and he sold himself to do evil.

טָמַן בְּלִבּוֹ מַחְשְׁבוֹת עֲרוּמָיו,
וַיִּתְמַכֵּר לַעֲשׂוֹת רָעָה.

י He raised his hand against God's holy ones, he gave his money to erase their memory.

יָדוֹ שָׁלַח בִּקְדוֹשֵׁי אֵ-ל, כַּסְפּוֹ
נָתַן לְהַכְרִית זִכְרָם.

Scavenger Hunt Answers

Chapter 1

1. In total 187 days: 180 for the important people in the countries under his rule, and 7 days for the people of Shushan (1:4–5)
2. Karpas! (1:6) Although here it refers to a kind of fabric.
3. Ahashverosh (1:3, 1:5) and Vashti (1:9)
4. The Megillah doesn't say why! (1:12)

Chapter 2

1. Kish (2:5)
2. Hadassah (2:7)
3. Every day (2:11)
4. In the 10th month (Tevet) of the 7th year of Ahashverosh's rule (2:16)

Chapter 3

1. 10,000 talents of silver (3:9)
2. His ring (3:10)
3. אֲחַשְׁדַּרְפְּנֵי הַמֶּלֶךְ (ahashdarpenei ha-melekh, the king's highest officers) (3:12)
4. The last pasuk in the chapter (3:15)

Chapter 4

1. That Mordekhai was wearing rags and ashes (4:1–4)
2. 30 days (4:11)
3. Whether Esther somehow became queen specifically so that she would one day be able to save the Jewish people (4:14)
4. Three days (4:16)

Chapter 5

1. Make a wooden post, and tell Ahashverosh to hang Mordekhai on it (5:14)
2. The wooden post; it was 50 amot tall (5:14)
3. To come with Haman to a banquet that day (5:4), and then for the two of them to come to another banquet the following day (5:8)
4. The next day (5:14)

Chapter 6

1. "Who's in the courtyard?" (6:4)
2. "This is what is done to a person whom the king wants to honor!" (6:11)
3. Haman (6:12)
4. That Haman will never be able to defeat Mordekhai (6:13)

Chapter 7

1. Be silent (7:4)
2. Because he was angry (7:7)
3. הָמָן (Haman), the note is called קַרְנֵי פָרָה (karnei farah, cows' horns) (7:9)
4. Harvonah (7:9)

Chapter 8

1. Mordekhai (8:2)
2. Nope! (8:8)
3. שֶׁבַע וְעֶשְׂרִים וּמֵאָה מְדִינָה וּמְדִינָה, which literally means something like: 127 provinces, every province and province (8:9)
4. Mordekhai (8:15)

Chapter 9

1. Because we're told וְנַהֲפוֹךְ הוּא (venahafokh hu, the opposite happened) (9:1)
2. Mordekhai (9:4)
3. דּוֹר וָדוֹר מִשְׁפָּחָה וּמִשְׁפָּחָה מְדִינָה וּמְדִינָה וְעִיר וָעִיר (generation to generation, family to family, province to province, city to city) (9:28)
4. Five times (9:26, 28, 29, 31, 32)

Chapter 10

1. The sea islands (10:1)
2. The History Book of the Kings of Madai and Persia (10:2)
3. He is second-in-command to Ahashverosh (10:3)

The Hadar Institute

Hadar empowers Jews to create and sustain vibrant, practicing, egalitarian communities of Torah, Avodah, and Hesed. Learn more at www.hadar.org.

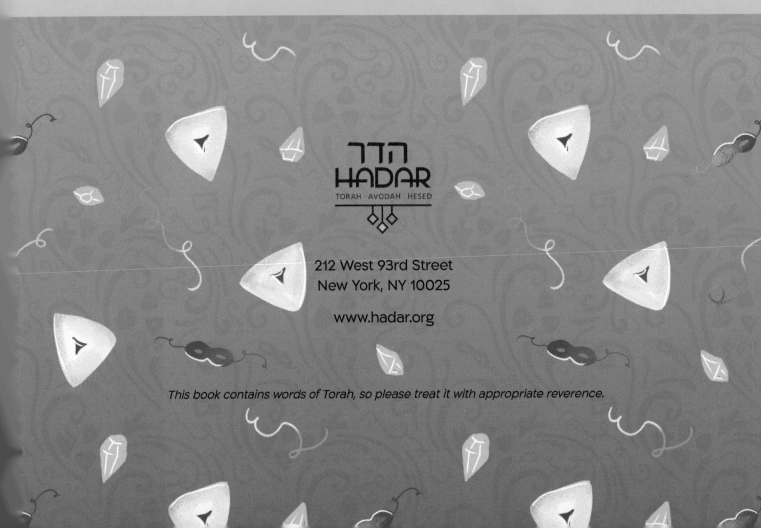

הדר
HADAR
TORAH · AVODAH · HESED

212 West 93rd Street
New York, NY 10025

www.hadar.org

This book contains words of Torah, so please treat it with appropriate reverence.